TRUE TALES, LEGENDS & LORE
——— OF THE ———
PECOS RIVER

JAMES COLLETT

THE
History
PRESS

Published by The History Press
Charleston, SC
www.historypress.com

First published 2024

Manufactured in the United States

ISBN 9781467157339

Library of Congress Control Number: 2024938214

To the Pecos River folks. You'll do to ride the river with!

CONTENTS

ACKNOWLEDGEMENTS

So many Pecos Country folks helped me with this book. I hope I can recall all of them. A special thanks to Denzel and Wayne Holmes, former Sheffield residents, for all sorts of help. Thanks to Victoria Contreras, Archives of the Big Bend, and Brenda Kizzar and Ellen Friar, Ward County Archives, for their assistance with many great photographs and resources in their files. Thanks to Jefferson Spillman, Fort Lancaster State Historic Site, for helping me with stories of the fort; to Ernest Woodward, Betty Damron, Delane Cagle and Kirby Warnock for their input and for bringing Horsehead Crossing alive again; to Melissa Hagins, director of Pecos Trail, for helping connect me with people and resources; and to Joe A. and Charlena Chandler for sharing a bit of their family's ranch history with me. Special thanks go to my children. Thanks, James Michael Collett, for all your feedback, your ideas and several of your photographs. Thanks, Jamie Thomason, for reading my often very rough drafts and providing feedback. Finally, my special heartfelt thanks to my greatest supporter, best friend and fellow adventurer in life, my wife, Jo Ann.

INTRODUCTION

I was born beside the Pecos River in a hospital in Iraan, Texas, amid the legendary Yates oil fields. I grew up in the hamlet of Sheffield, just over the hill from Pecos Spring. I drank from it more than once. My great-grandfather pioneered a ranch along the river's banks that remains in the family. Generations of my family lived somewhere along the river—some still do.

As a youngster, I swam in the Pecos, tasting its brackish water in my mouth. I fished the green alkaline waters with a cane pole, catching shiny perch or an occasional gar. For years, I rode a yellow school bus along the river to school in Iraan. During my teaching career at McCamey, former oil boomtown and stop on the Orient Railroad, the Pecos was always there, meandering a few miles to the south and west.

Countless times, I wandered the banks of the Pecos seeking traces of ancient Native Americans—the remains of their campsites, pieces of their stone tools—or scrambled up nearby mesas to search out rock art they left in shallow limestone hollows. I have seen and smelled the river up close from a tangle of mesquite and salt cedar and viewed panoramic sweeps of its path from atop mesas and canyon rims. I have seen times so dry the riverbed caught fire and so wet the old river raged a mile wide, flooding anything in its path. The river is an integral piece of my history. I cannot recount my story without it. It has always been there, a marker in the landscape of my life.

From prehistoric times, the Pecos and its watershed have played a significant role in the lives of any who ventured there. This is a land of contradictions, at times life-giving, inspiring reverence—a destructive, killing force at others.

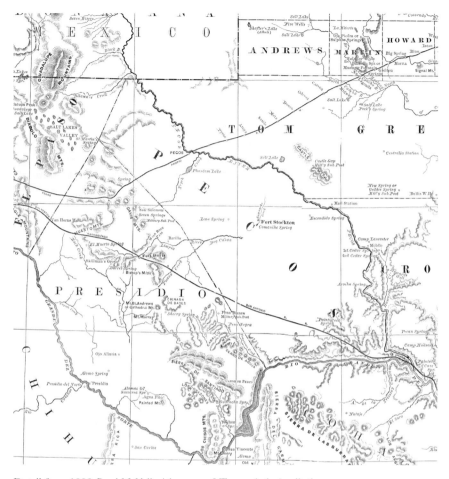

Detail from 1882 *Rand McNally Atlas* map of Texas. *Author's collection.*

Many found a home along its banks—Native Americans, farmers and ranchers, a variety of entrepreneurs, townsfolk and sportsmen. Some made a new beginning here. Others, like outlaws, vanished. The river provided a pathway across an arid, desolate landscape. It formed a dangerous, challenging barrier to journeys. More than once, the river valley has been a violently contested space where armies and cultures clashed. On its long journey through time and space, the Pecos has accumulated a rich collection of great tales. Some are dramatic, some tragic, some heroic and a few even epic. Many are grounded in facts, others solidly rooted in fantasy. All have contributed to the mythic image of Texas and the American West. This book contains a few of them.

RIVER IN THE DESERT

Desert rivers are not easy to love. Some carry acrid waters, their sparse vegetation providing little shelter or sustenance as they meander across alkaline floodplains. Others carve deep, nearly impenetrable channels through rocky terrain, creating impassable barriers. On its journey across Texas, the Pecos River does both.

The Pecos enters Texas at the upper end of the Red Bluff Reservoir, constructed in 1936. From there, it draws a winding diagonal path across Texas to meet the Rio Grande, slicing away the triangular western end of the state, bestowing its name on that vast region: the Trans-Pecos.

The river arrives in the state heavily loaded with salty water. Much of the brine comes from saline springs flowing into the river as it traverses the horseshoe-shaped Malaga Bend south of Loving, New Mexico. Just below the Red Bluff Reservoir, Salt Creek adds more salinity. Downriver from the town of Pecos, Texas, Toyah Creek carries the brackish waters of Toyah Lake to the river. Underground seepage leaks more salt into the river.

The brine-laden river sinuously wanders across a relatively level, barren, dusty plain, twisting and turning almost back on itself like some lost soul. It cuts a channel, lined with frequently steep and treacherous earth banks often devoid of vegetation that can unexpectedly surprise someone approaching it. One account tells of the cowboy who crossed the river to recover a cow only to find that the animal had been on his side all along.

The river's peregrinations eventually carry it into the West Texas mesas. King Mountain and Southwest Mesa push it westward until Tunas Creek along the base of Indian Mesa helps herd it eastward. Near Iraan, the river

Pecos River near McCamey, Texas. *Photograph by author.*

encounters the western edge of the Edwards Plateau and is driven south by that limestone barrier into a broad canyon flanked with terraced mesa lands hundreds of feet high. From here to the Rio Grande, the valley will only grow narrower and steeper. South of Iraan, the Pecos shifts back and forth across the valley, sometimes cutting away a mountain's end, leaving rocky bluffs.

Pecos Spring at Sheffield sends a bit of fresh water into the saline river, as do Live Oak and Independence Creeks downriver. Although its water is relatively clear, with an aquamarine tint, the Pecos never fully sheds its bitter taste. The river's path straightens, somewhat, although the Pecos will still cut winding turns through the mesas and narrowing rock walls.

The lower Pecos takes on a completely different nature. From Pandale, where the broad Howard Draw empties into the Pecos at a rocky crossing, the river enters some fifty miles of steep, jagged limestone walls, hundreds of feet high, filled with challenging whitewater passages, bony limestone channels known as the Flutes and reed-lined rocky banks until the Pecos finally meets the Rio Grande and its rocky gorge, just beyond the two spectacular Pecos High Bridges.

The view of the mouth of the Pecos at the U.S. Highway 90 overlook is so vastly and dramatically different than the one from the bridge at Texas Highway 302 just west of Mentone that it is easy to understand why early mapmakers often failed to connect the two portions of the river.

"PECOS"

Over the past few centuries, the word *Pecos* has acquired a considerable range of meanings and connotations. It has been a noun, a verb, a description, a landscape, a boundary and, of course, a river made mythically ominous. While many of these varied terms have largely passed from common usage, their vestiges remain.

Even the origin of the river's name has multiple variations. A logical one is that "Pecos" derives from the Keresan (Native American language) term for the Pecos Pueblo, *p'æyok'ona*. A bit more removed, *pecus* is the Latin term for a single head of cattle. The Spanish had no term for the buffalo and referred to them as cows, more often as *vaca* however. Further afield is the idea the word comes from *puerco*, a Spanish term for pig. However, *puerco* can also mean something "foul" or "nasty." Puerco was among the early names given the river and is certainly an apt description for the alkaline stream, although it requires some convolutions to become "pecos." Along with "Puerco," the river bore another early name, "Rio Salado" or "Salty River," that also definitely fits its Texas course. Finally, *pecoso*, meaning "spotted," produces even more head scratching.

However it received its name, the dangerous river soon lent its name to sinister actions. To "pecos" someone meant to kill them and throw the body in the river or, more generally, to kill someone wherever. A "pecos swap" became a euphemism for stealing. "West of the Pecos" became synonymous with a wild, lawless realm.

When the term became a person's nickname, "Pecos" endowed the individual with a special status, someone out of the ordinary, perhaps a highly skilled horseman or someone more deadly with a gun. Anytime the name appears in an old western movie, the viewer should immediately recognize that this is an important and complex character, often a "good badman."

Some connotations probably gained strength from associations with the early history of the community of Pecos, originally Pecos City. Known as a roughhewn town, filled with cowboys and saloons, it claims to have originated the first modern rodeo. In the late 1800s, dangerous men walked its streets, among them Clay Allison, Blackjack Ketchum, Jim Miller and perhaps even John Wesley Hardin. The Orient Bar hosted a classic gunfight. All fuel for a deadly "pecos."

The 1930s helped solidify the river's image. J. Frank Dobie devoted a chapter of *Coronado's Children*, his 1930 book of the folklore of lost treasures, to the "Pecos Barricade." Zane Grey's novel *West of the Pecos* came out in 1937, filled with mythic "Pecos" allusion, including the character Pecos Smith, who has "pecosed" several men by the end of the novel. The year 1936 brought the Texas Centennial, enhancing the mythic image of the Lone Star State to entice more travelers to venture along the burgeoning highway system. That same year, J. Evetts Haley's biography *Charles Goodnight: Cowman and Plainsman* was published, containing Goodnight's quote defining the Pecos as "the graveyard of the cowman's hopes." Ranchers along the river are still wary of the treacherous mud, which can deeply mire an animal, requiring great effort to free them without harm.

In more recent times, the word has gained new associations. The "Lower Pecos" now references float trips down the river below Pandale or the prehistoric culture that produced world-class rock art in that same region. Pecos cantaloupes claim to be world-renowned. Photographs of the Pecos High Bridge are among the most iconic images of the state. Even in a digital world far removed from the days of Native Americans, Spaniards and cowboys, "Pecos" still produces echoes of legendary places and people.

ANCIENT LIVES

Walk almost any mile of the Texas Pecos River, even the more desolate ones, and you will encounter traces left behind by those who lived along its banks in long-passed centuries. These remains are mostly rough fist-sized chunks of gray stones scattered about or piled in rocky heaps mixed with ash-smeared earth. Among those lie sharp-edged, shiny fragments of flint, or chert, glittering like broken glass in the sunlight. Most are a plain gray color, but bits of yellow, brown, black and dark red are visible as well.

These are remains of the lives of the Native Americans who dwelt in the Pecos Country for some nine thousand years. The softer, more organic remnants of their lives—food, clothing, sandals, wooden tools—have long since decayed, except for a fragile few buried in the detritus of shallow rock shelters. Mostly, only the stones remain.

We can never know these people. The daily details of their lives. The names they called themselves; the ones they gave one another. Their thoughts and dreams and the stories they handed down. We can see and touch and know the work of their hands, however. It remains, embedded in the memory of the stones they fired, chipped or painted. We will never know them, but the stones knew them. The stones still carry their memory.

The Musk Hog People

Travelers cruising Interstate 10 may hardly realize when they cross the Pecos River, with only a small sign and low parapet marking the spot. Few show interest in the swath of emerald-tinted water flowing sluggishly between earth banks sparse with vegetation.

East of the river, on the western edge of the Edwards Plateau, the road follows Musk Hog Canyon as it curves two miles to its head six hundred feet above the river. There is nothing visible to inform passing motorists that they are crossing a landscape filled with remains of ancient lives lived here that was nominated to the National Register of Historic Places.

The mesa lands of West Texas consist of relatively flat limestone tablelands covered with a thin, rocky dirt mantle. Drainages carve into the rock, creating narrow canyons that join others, widening into larger valleys. Along their edges, eroded limestone forms a caprock pockmarked with shallow depressions. The hills slope steeply, stairstepping level by level to the canyon floors, where the soil becomes thicker. The land is rich in outcrops of flint, a quartz-like stone that fractures into sharp pieces of varying size. Vegetation includes scrubby junipers, small clusters of hackberry and mountain laurel, scattered grasses, mesquite, sotol, lechuguilla, prickly pear cactus and yucca. Thin along the slopes, the flora increases in the canyon bottoms. Wildlife includes rabbits, deer, doves, hawks, vultures, a variety of rodents, snakes and insects, as well as fish and mussels in the river. The buffalo are gone, but they have come and gone before.

In 1971, the proposed route of Interstate 10 was surveyed through Musk Hog Canyon. Archaeologists found several hearths, the rock-lined remains of Native American campfires and burned rock middens, donut-shaped piles of fire-cracked rock marking ancient plant-baking activities. Before construction began, the Texas Archaeological Society (TAS) held its 1976 field school in Musk Hog. The goal was to survey the entire canyon for a larger-scale perspective of prehistoric life in the region. Professionals and amateur volunteers spent a week seeking remaining traces of prehistoric human activity. By the end of that June week, they had found more than five hundred sites. Hearths, burned rock middens, smoke-stained rock shelters, flint quarry sites and a handful of red and yellow faded pictographs were all there in Musk Hog.

Using what they found, archaeologists reconstructed the story of life in Musk Hog across the centuries. Prehistoric time in the Pecos Country has been divided into three broad categories, marking changes in climate

View of Musk Hog Canyon from the Pecos River Valley. *Photograph by author.*

and lifeways. The oldest is the Paleoindian, reaching back eight thousand years or more before the present. Next, the Archaic is a great swath of time from the Paleo years to 700 CE (the Common Era, in which we live). The Late Prehistoric (from 700 CE to historic times) includes important developments—the bow and arrow, pottery and new tools of a bison-hunting culture.

Only a few souls ventured into Musk Hog late in the Paleo period, perhaps pursuing the last of Pleistocene fauna—mammoth, huge bison, camels, horses, sloths—all now extinct.

Across the long Archaic, Musk Hog was home to small kinship groups, as few as a dozen, as many as seventy, generation after generation. They lived across the lower reaches of the canyon, hunting small game and foraging from the landscape. In winters, they moved uphill into the rock shelters. The canyon's limited resources, then much as they are now, made them nomadic. Musk Hog became part of a broader region they considered their domain. They wandered it, seeking what they needed in a seasonal pattern for five thousand years.

Even in this slowly changing world, things changed. Four thousand years ago, the climate grew increasingly arid. Resources became scarcer. The nomadic people were forced to find new food sources. Among these were the large bulbs and the base of the lechuguilla and sotol. The tough, fibrous plants, baked in large earth ovens, became a necessary food source, not a delicacy. So did land snails, eaten in far greater numbers. Middens of blackened, fire-cracked rock grew across the canyon.

About 2,500 years ago, things improved. The climate became cooler and wetter. The grasslands thickened and spread. So did the bison, drifting south into the Musk Hog country. The nomads crafted new tools to hunt and process this new quarry. Those good days were relatively short-lived, perhaps 1,000 years, before the climate resumed its path toward the arid world we know today. Baking ovens returned. The people also turned to the Pecos, taking fish and mussels from the river. Piles of shells joined those of fire-cracked rock. Some of them they shaped into shiny pieces of jewelry.

An invention, the bow, appeared 1,300 years ago. A bison-hunting culture spread west from Central Texas, disrupting centuries-old territorial boundaries. Arrows killed more than game. By the time the Spaniards wandered the river they called the Salado, they encountered no one in Musk Hog Canyon.

Musk Hog is not unique, however, only better known from the opportunity Interstate 10 created for archaeologists. Almost any canyon in the Pecos Country contains a version of this story.

If you pass through Musk Hog Canyon some late evening, stop a moment to stand beside your vehicle and listen. Beyond the noise of passing vehicles, you will hear only silence. No one lives there; no one has for centuries. Many once did. Only silent, rocky traces remain to speak for them.

Hearth

As I descended the ridge, I tried to reimagine the site below as it appeared when a fire still burned in the hearth. The small ridge of sandy dirt where it lay extended closer to the creek bed. There was no mesquite, only a grove of live oak trees, like those still flourishing along the creek named for them. Water trickled or gurgled a few steps from the campsite. Upstream, the large pool beneath the metate-strewn shelf of rock held fish and watery vegetation. The level skyline of mesas framing the horizon was the same.

Shelters of wood and brush hides formed a small cluster, extending along the soft soil bank of the creek. The accumulations of daily life lay scattered about, delineating the boundaries of the camp. And there, beside one shelter housing its builders, a soft glimmer of red and yellow, draped in a gossamer veil of wood smoke in the evening light, sent out the warm message of home to those returning.

Twelve miles east of the Pecos River, Interstate 10 crosses Live Oak Creek, an intermittent stream that carries fresh water south into the salty river. On a Saturday in May 2001, seven Iraan Archaeological Society members braved the heat that had scorched West Texas for two weeks to return to a spot on the bank of the creek a few hundred yards downstream from the interstate. The objective was to uncover six rocks buried in the creek bank. During a field trip the previous month, the group had discovered these stones, which appeared to mark the edge of a buried hearth.

A small shower of rain fell as the team arrived at the site, and a cloud cover kept the temperature pleasant for most of the morning. Wasting little time, we set out to discover what lay beneath the soil. Within an hour, the team uncovered an almost intact hearth, a bowl-shaped group of rocks about two feet across. The irregular limestone cobbles were local, carried a short distance to construct this artifact. As we brushed away the soil to expose the bottom layer of stone, the black remains of the last fires to warm this hearth glittered darkly before fading once exposed to the morning light.

At first, the stones appeared roughly laid, the gaps between them filled with ash and dirt. However, further cleaning revealed almost all fitted closely together underneath, their irregular shapes allowing for the fill accumulation. A thinner ring of stones dressed the top of the hearth. Photographs were taken during the dig of the exposed hearth, and scale drawings were made. Samples of ash were collected for possible later carbon dating. The completeness of this hearth fascinated us. Most found in the Pecos River terrain were badly eroded or deflated.

We posed beside the excavated hearth and then reburied it in the soil that had long protected it. We left with renewed respect for the resourcefulness of these prehistoric neighbors who knew this land long before us.

The Spanish word for hearth, *hogar*, can also mean home. This small group of stones—so artfully, one can even argue lovingly, arranged—provided a center place for a family, possibly even generations of families, returning over the years. Beside it, they shared warmth, food and companionship.

They shared far more, however. They shared the moments of the day, their plans for the coming days, their memories, their musings, their tall tales, their legends and myths and their knowledge—in fact, everything. In a society without writing, lacking the ability to store information in more than the human mind, *everything* was transmitted orally across generations or was

Iraan Archaeological Society members beside the excavated hearth. *Photograph by author.*

irretrievably lost. How to build a hearth. How to form a stone tool. What plants to eat, to use as medicine, to avoid and where to find them. What is dangerous. What is deadly. Who to marry and who to avoid. Tales about ancestors. How things came to be. Rules, rituals, beliefs. Everything! That small hearth represented an entire shared worldview.

During the excavation that overcast day, I removed my sunglasses and forgot them. I received permission to return a few days later to retrieve them.

Walking in from the ranch road, I tried to imagine the site as it appeared when that fire burned. I may have done a better job of it than I thought. By the time I reached the buried hearth, the day was fading into evening, the twilight moving fast toward darkness. The glasses lay where I had left them, covered with a thin film of dust. As I stepped closer to pick them up, I felt the most intense sensation down into my bones that I had stepped into someone's "home," in their still lived-in space. As if they were just away along the creek somewhere, perhaps on the last forage of the day, and would soon return to the evening fire. To this hearth. It was not frightening, just intensely personal. A memory shared from someone else's remembered earth.

THE WHITE SHAMAN

You approach the small rock shelter from below, just as the ancient pilgrims did, climbing the steep limestone slope to reach this hollow just beneath the narrow canyon rim. Of course, the stairway of stone steps and the chain strung on poles embedded in the rock were not there. Otherwise, the terrain is the same as it was some three thousand years ago when this place became a sacred space.

At the top of the stairs, a curved, rocky alcove creates a sixty-five-foot amphitheater with a stunning view to the southwest of the meeting of the Pecos and Rio Grande. The Pecos High Bridge outlines a modern pattern of horizontal and vertical concrete and metal lines across this landscape, spanning the space between the steep rocky canyon walls.

Several shallow ledges provide natural seating in the rocky recess. Where the shelter curves around to the south, the upper half of the wall contains what has brought visitors to this spot for centuries. A fascinating and bewildering assemblage of images some twenty-six feet long and thirteen feet high fills that space. As breathtaking as the view to the south it faces, this profusion of figures spreads across the rocky wall, painted in four colors—black, red, yellow, and white—117 of them in all.

A ghostly figure near the center gave the site its current name, the White Shaman mural. Photographer Jim Zintgraff and archaeologist Solveig Turpin saw this floating headless image, painted largely in white, as a shaman figure, a special individual capable of entering mind-altering trances, often with hallucinogenic aid, to travel into spiritual worlds. To them, this artistic array depicted a shamanic odyssey.

When artist and photographer Carolyn Boyd first visited the White Shaman cave, she saw a single composition, requiring a tremendous amount of preparation and skill. She had little idea what the painting meant but knew that she was viewing something extraordinary. Boyd spent the next three decades of her life—as an artist, as an anthropologist, as a scientist—studying this artwork in microscopic detail (literally, with an electron microscope) to discover just how extraordinary it was. She founded the Shumla Archaeological Research and Education Center in nearby Comstock and recruited other experts to join her undertaking. They brought specialized tools—including photographic software, laser mapping scanners, digital microscopes and computers—for an in-depth analysis. Coupled with the scientific study, Boyd researched the mythology of Mesoamerica for clues. The results produced a fantastic story.

View of the Pecos River from White Shaman Shelter. *Photograph by author.*

As a single composition, the entire panel's vision was completed in the artists' minds before applying the first stroke of paint. Microscopic study revealed that the paint colors were applied separately, in a highly specific order. Black paint was used first, in three layers, correctly placed to fit the final mural. Next came five red layers, then two yellow ones and, finally, two layers of white. Animal fat provided the paint's bonding agent. Sacrificing this important calorie source, challenging to acquire in the ancient Trans-Pecos, for artwork, signified the importance of this work.

Boyd's ethnographic studies led her to Huichol mythology. The Huichol still live in relative isolation in mountainous western Mexico, their beliefs and traditions changed little since pre-Columbian times. They still conduct ritual pilgrimages to collect peyote, guided by the spirit of the sacred deer, also a peyote symbol. When Boyd compared elements of the Huichol rituals and mythology to the White Shaman mural, she found unmistakable correspondences. She bolstered these with historic and archaeological records of the Nahua (the Aztec), whom the Spanish encountered in central Mexico.

In *The White Shaman Mural*, Boyd presents the argument that this mural is a kind of codex like those made in pre-Columbian Mesoamerica. These were "books" that conveyed their information in graphic form instead of written language. Boyd claims, "Nothing about the White Shaman mural is random." Every element of it is part of a complex narrative. For her, this painting is the oldest known "book" in North America.

The narrative within this "book" contains multiple meanings and functions. It is a creation story, recounting the birth of the sun and the dawn of time. It presented the details for ritually reenacting this event. Finally, it provided a visible message to the Native community communicating how the eternal and the supernatural were tangibly present in their world. A modern Huichol priest, viewing the mural through tear-filled eyes, asserted, "This is our creation myth."

Five heroic figures, the original mythical peyote deer hunters, set out on the peyote hunt, carrying torches to enter the underworld. Their journey unfolds across the painting, through a bewildering multitude of interwoven images, interacting in a cosmic dance. Arches, lines, black dots. Atlatls. Human figures, rising or falling headlong. Deer pierced by darts. Fantastical creatures. On the far right, almost lost in the artistic profusion, the tiny, humanized figure of the sun rides forth on the Morning Star, transformed into a deer.

And the white shaman? Boyd views her as the decapitated moon goddess, dressed in white, who arose from the ashes of creation. Her S-shaped serpent

The White Shaman mural. *Photograph by author.*

arrows represent her association with the rain serpent of the west and the winter solstice.

Written words fail at describing this artwork. Photographs as well. They frame—they limit the view. To gain any true appreciation of this complex, multidimensional graphic work of art, this "book," one must stand before it where it was produced and where it exists, in a rock shelter overlooking the mouth of the Pecos River. And then, only through a glass, darkly. Standing in a world of different mythologies, a nearby modern engineering marvel disrupting the ancient view, we will never fully comprehend the White Shaman mural as the living thing it once was. Yet even this limited glimpse leaves any visitor with a feeling of awe, a sense of having stood in sacred space.

The White Shaman mural is owned by the Witte Museum of San Antonio. Guided tours of the White Shaman site are regularly available, but reservations are required.

LEAP OF DEATH

By the time the bull realized that the drop was there, it was too late. As he frantically attempted to stop, the frightened bison behind collided with him, and they all plunged into the canyon. Their massive bodies smashed into a jumbled pile of rocks below and tumbled into the shallow limestone cave at the base of the canyon wall. Many died on impact or beneath a crush of bodies. Survivors bellowed in pain and fright, broken limbs grotesquely splayed.

The hunters moved in, carefully avoiding thrashing horns and hooves, dispatching those animals still alive with stone axes and knives. As the dying noises faded, they began expertly butchering the animals. The jump had worked excellently. Everyone would eat well for a long while.

This scene played out almost twelve thousand years ago at a place now known as Bonfire Shelter. It lies near the head of Mile Canyon, a narrow ravine carved deeply through the limestone bedrock that empties into the Rio Grande just east of the small town of Langtry. Unless one knows where to look when crossing it on Highway 90, you would not know the crescent-shaped shelter was there. That is a good thing because this virtually hidden spot preserves the remains of a remarkable event, the earliest bison jump site in North America, as well as the one farthest south. It also lies on private property, and the owners are highly protective of this unique place.

Bonfire Shelter. *Photograph by author.*

The term "bison jump" refers to the coordinated effort of a group of prehistoric Native Americans to drive a herd of bison over the edge of a precipice to their death. This required maneuvering a group of the gregarious creatures toward the intended drop, usually not visible very far from the edge. Once the herd was properly positioned, hunters stampeded them, using fire and noise or waving blankets. Other hunters along the route leaped up and added to the beasts' panic. Artificial rock or brush barriers helped channel the route of the animals. If all went as intended, the bison reached the edge of the cliff unable to stop and plunged over.

Several bison jumps have been identified across North America. However, all are located on the northern Great Plains, in Montana and Canada. No others are known this far south, especially this old. Bonfire Shelter is twice as old as any other identified jumps. Even the creatures they killed are more ancient than those at other sites.

In 1958, a high school student walked up to "Ice Box" Cave (as it was then called for always being a cooler spot in the canyon) in search of prehistoric stone artifacts. He dug into a thick layer of large, charred bone remains. Curiosity about what he found helped fuel the desire of this student to become an archaeologist. Years later, Dr. Michael B. Collins, a well-known expert in Paleoindian archaeology, returned to extensively study the lower Pecos prehistoric cultures.

Interest in Collins's find as a student launched a series of archaeological digs over the next few decades in the renamed Bonfire Shelter. That name derives from at least two conflagrations produced by spontaneous combustion of the decaying carcasses of so many bison. As the different excavation teams worked, a tale of not one but multiple jumps, centuries apart, emerged.

The archaeological teams uncovered three layers of bones. The layer closest to the surface, Bone Bed Three, contained an extensive collection of burned bone fragments, representing several hundred modern bison (*Bison bison*), killed during the Late Archaic period (from 3,000 to 1,300 years ago). Stone points among the bones established the time frame for one or more jumps.

The kills represented a tremendous source of food to the people involved, even with the larger number of people required for a successful jump. A single large modern bison bull weighs as much as a ton (2,240 pounds) and stands six feet high. The butchering process would have taken weeks to complete. As the animals were processed, most of the work was probably done out on the canyon floor as the stench of bloated animals grew. The carcasses were cut open for favored parts—tongues, brains, stomach contents. The major meat pieces—forequarters, hindquarters and backstraps—were cut apart and carried outside. To take full advantage of such a volume of meat, much of it would have been sun-dried or smoked. Hides would have been stripped away and processed. Skulls or other special bones may have become ritual pieces.

A few feet below Bone Bed Three, excavators discovered Bone Bed Two. However, these bones, representing 120 animals, were those of the extinct bison (*Bison antiquus*), creatures at least 15 percent larger than the modern species. The animals perished in three separate bison jumps at least 11,300 years ago. Carcasses of the earliest of these most likely caused the first of the shelter's bonfires.

Years of archaeological work at Bonfire Shelter have established the case that it represents the earliest bison jump in North America. For many years, it was believed that such a feat was beyond the ability of the small families of nomadic hunter-gatherers in the area at that time. A growing body of evidence and the bones in the shelter prove that this was not the case.

As I drive through the Pecos country around Bonfire Shelter, I enjoy imagining the landscape when the massive, hairy *Bison antiquus* roamed there. And the sound and smell and dust and exuberant energy as those ancient people chased them to their death.

I ponder one other thought. Did those later hunters running the descendants of the ancient bison over the rim of Mile Canyon have any memory that they were re-creating an event achieved by their ancestors millennia before? Did they rediscover the concept and site of the jump themselves, or were they inspired by some ancient mythical tale of feats and feasts told across the campfires of time?

Carving Magic in Stone

When you first view it, the limestone ledge looks like numerous others lining the rim of the Lower Pecos canyonlands. Steep hundred-foot drop-offs frame the flat expanse on two sides. On the south, Lewis Canyon, a sixteen-mile intermittent tributary, reaches the Pecos from the east. To the west, the sheer drop is to the Pecos. The site is bounded by low rocky hills on the north and east. Other than scattered clumps of native grass, a few ocotillos, tasajillos and prickly pear have taken root.

As you walk onto the limestone bedrock, you quickly see what makes this spot unique. More than nine hundred designs have been pecked into the rock. Most are a profusion of geometric figures. There are curving lines, often in pairs or groupings; coiled circles; and numerous lines running through pecked circles. Here and there are a few recognizable shapes: human figures (including a "lizard man"), deer tracks, a human footprint and a single handprint. They appear to have no unifying pattern.

Only one spot hints at a story, a six-foot line with thirty-five short perpendicular tabs along it, ending in a hook. It runs between a pair of bear tracks, with two of the stick and circle figures beside it. Archaeologists believe that these repeating images represent atlatls, a dart-throwing weapon that preceded the bow. Based on when the bow is believed to have arrived in the Lower Pecos region, this makes the carvings more than 1,000 to 1,300 years old. Is this perhaps a bear hunt story? Or something else?

What makes the Lewis Canyon petroglyphs so extraordinary is that they are an anomaly in the landscape. While the canyons in this region are filled with a wealth of colorful and elaborate art painted on the walls of rock shelters, there is not another similar petroglyph site here or far beyond, across West Texas and northeastern Mexico. Seventy years of searching

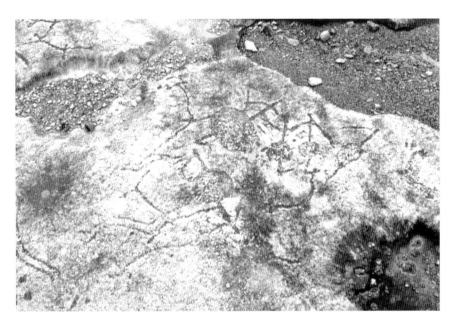

Lewis Canyon petroglyphs. *Courtesy of James Michael Collett.*

have failed to find any comparable body of petroglyphs in the region. There is nothing like it. Nothing.

As archaeologists and rock art crews visited and studied the site, they developed theories explaining what all this carving, requiring a significant amount of effort, might mean and why it was placed in this particular spot.

Prehistoric art almost always reflects some aspect of the cultural system producing it, especially when themes and elements are created repeatedly. Something was being symbolically communicated that held meaning understood by the people of that society. All the images elaborately pecked into this rock made it into a sacred space.

One common theory is that this art is some form of hunting magic. At Lewis Canyon, the most commonly interpretable carving is the atlatl or spear thrower, the most formidable weapon of its time. In many carvings, the stone weight, or bannerstone, that provided extra power to the throw is exaggerated as a large circular excision near the middle of the shaft.

The sinuous lines and circles may represent some trance or vision state. Research has established that altered states of consciousness, whether produced by hallucinogenic drugs or trance states, produce the same basic set of visual images among all humans. Lewis Canyon, on this platform elevated above the river and open to sun and night sky, could represent a place of communication with the supernatural, especially when viewed holistically from above. Reasonable assumptions, but again, why only here?

As the rock art recording crews removed dirt that eroded onto the site over the centuries, they uncovered a key to the answer. Shallow, sinuous erosion channels cut paths across the gently sloping bedrock. Many of them eventually connect to a large tinaja, or bedrock tank, forty-five feet long and up to fifteen feet wide, that was also once fed by an underground flow. When heavy rains filled the tinaja to capacity, it would hold about eight hundred gallons. The overflow would run down a shallow channel to the river. Heavy downpours in the Lower Pecos produce rapid and dramatic waterfalls that plunge down the cliffs beside the petroglyphs and pour into the river.

Prehistoric people have a universal reverence for water, especially subterranean water. Thus, the curving lines across the bedrock, when paired or grouped, may connect magically to the erosion channels. The numerous powerful atlatls would add ritual strength to this place, although the exact logic how lies beyond us.

Water was the focus. Not only water for the body, but also water for the spirit. Water became the means to communicate with spirits in the rock, the earth and in the sky above. When the rains came and the water flowed over the rock into the tinaja and, at times, over the sheer cliff walls, cascading into the river, this became a "thin place" where the rim of the Pecos touched the rim of the supernatural.

ROUTES WEST

The end of the United States war with Mexico in 1848 and the discovery of gold in California produced a growing demand for routes west across Texas to the gold fields. Several reconnaissance expeditions wandered across the Trans-Pecos, eventually mapping two routes. These would become the Lower Road from San Antonio to El Paso and, later, the Emigrant's Road, which crossed the Pecos at Horsehead Crossing. Over the next century, even as transportation changed, the paths of railroads and automobiles frequently followed these trailblazing efforts.

ROAD TO THE PECOS

In June 1849, the Third U.S. Infantry Regiment received orders assigning it to duty in New Mexico. To reach there, the troops constructed a route across West Texas to the Pecos River and beyond to El Paso. What they built became the Lower or Military Road.

To achieve this project, an immense wagon train—more than three hundred wagons strong, including nine hundred soldiers, teamsters and a road-building crew—headed west from San Antonio. In addition to two hundred quartermaster wagons and seventy wagons of regimental baggage, there were army sutler wagons and carts and miscellaneous other vehicles, including several army ambulances. Three thousand animals—horses, mules and oxen—pulled the vast assemblage.

From the Leona River, the long train followed the progress made by the road building crew commanded by Lieutenant Colonel Joseph Johnston. Third Infantry soldiers sometimes assisted with road building, and in the early days, civilians from San Antonio even volunteered. The road ran in a straight line across the open prairie for the 170 miles to the Devils River.

The road building grew increasingly challenging as the route wound up the Devils River, then across the Edwards Plateau to the Pecos. Using picks, shovels and axes, the crew cut through the heavy brush, built passable grades across arroyos and constantly removed loose rocks from the road. The livestock required constant re-shoeing in the rocky terrain. The seventy-five miles from the head of the Devils River to the Pecos River took three weeks to complete.

At the western edge of the Edwards Plateau, the road crew built a steep six-hundred-foot descent to Live Oak Creek and the Pecos River Valley. They carved a narrow ledge from the limestone outcrops of the canyon walls, piling the rock along the outer edge as a berm. When finished, the road descended at an angle so frighteningly precipitous that one Third Infantry officer remarked it appeared to those riding behind that the ones they were following "had drapt into the bowels of the earth." Many travelers who used this descent chose to lock their wheels rather than risk a runaway crash.

View down the Lower Road at Lancaster Hill in the early 1900s. Photograph by J. Stokley Ligon. *Archives of the Big Bend.*

The road continued to the Pecos, where a suitable ford was located. Beyond the Pecos, challenges continued. The temperature rose above 106 degrees in the shade. Wagons and equipment required constant repairs. Water, wood and adequate forage for animals were persistent problems. Native Americans trailed the party, stealing stock when opportunities presented themselves.

One hundred days after their departure from San Antonio, the expedition reached El Paso. The Lower Road was open for traffic. Thousands of gold seekers, travelers, stage line passengers and federal troops traveled this road for the next decade.

THE FIRST CATTLE DRIVES

Most Texas cattle drive accounts are post–Civil War ones moving north to railroad shipping points or markets in New Mexico and beyond. The first long cattle drives in Texas, however, pushed westward to the California gold fields. The multitude of miners and mining communities created a tremendous demand for beef. The delivery method available was to drive the hardy longhorn cattle the 1,500 miles to the gold fields.

An undocumented story claims that T.J. Trimmier made the first drive to California in 1848 with five hundred beeves, which he sold for $100 per head. On his return journey, he met multiple herds headed west. For the next dozen years, thousands of Texas longhorns, horses and mules streamed to California, reaching a peak by 1854.

Among those outfits trailing west that year was one owned by San Antonio pioneer surveyor and businessman John James. James assembled a large party for protection, including emigrants planning to remain on the West Coast. Twenty-two-year-old James G. Bell was one of these. Bell kept a diary of the journey, sending segments back to family members instead of letters. These were handed down through the family, and western historian J. Evetts Haley located them in 1932, publishing the Texas portion in the *Southwestern Historical Quarterly* journal that same year.

The James outfit departed San Antonio on the Lower Road on the evening of June 3, 1854. Greenhorn Bell managed to lose his mule that first evening, locating it after an hour's search. Otherwise, the early days of the journey were uneventful and pleasant.

The drive reached the Devils River at noon on the fifteenth and started upstream. A guide informed Bell that they would cross the river fourteen times over the next ten days. Bell visited one of the painted caves prevalent in the Lower Pecos country, commenting, "Probably this was a place of revelry."

Devils River travel proved challenging. The constant crossings of the cobblestoned riverbed were hard on the cattle's hooves. The danger of Indian attack increased. On the seventeenth, they passed two heaps of stones marking graves. James ordered no one to leave the train on their own. Camping away from the river, they found "poor soil, no grass, [and] poor mesquite." They reached a small posting of soldiers near the future site of Camp Hudson, where they rested the cattle for two days in preparation for a forty-mile trek without water.

The drive to the next water at Howard's Well took twenty grueling hours. Bell was part of the wagon escort. They reached the well at 3:00 a.m., hours behind the cattle. Following another rest day, they set out across the divide for Live Oak Creek, reaching it on midafternoon of the twenty-fifth. After describing the beautiful weather and expanse of "hill and plane," Bell noted that "the serious business of the trip is about to commence—that of standing guard, and a possibility of an attack from the Indians."

The next day, they reached the Pecos, which Bell recorded as "turbulent and rapid" and a bright, rich pink color. Although he mentions the banks being high and dangerous for cattle, he records no difficulties in crossing the animals. Two miles upstream, in the vicinity of Pecos Spring, they found a thicket of wild plums. Many of the crew took advantage of the opportunity to bathe but found the water muddy and "filthy for drinking and cooking."

The herd trailed along the Pecos the next three days. They passed several heaps of broken, fire-marked stones. Having no idea that these were burned rock cooking middens, Bell concluded that they must be used "to offer up sacrifices in time of battle or at death." He also speculated on possible treasures. "An exploration geologically would no doubt develop inexhaustible mines of gold, silver, copper, and iron." On the last day of June, they gladly left the Pecos for Escondido Springs and Comanche Springs beyond.

The remaining journey to El Paso became the most difficult part of the Texas trek. A herd a few days ahead had a firefight with Indians, killing several. The James party passed through the ambush spot of Wild Rose Pass without incident, however. The eighty-mile trek without water proved costly. Dust-covered, they pushed the livestock day and night. More than one hundred animals perished from exhaustion and thirst. Others wandered away in search of water. Bell pitied the suffering cattle but recognized that "they are compelled to go forward or die."

The James drive finally reached the Rio Grande on July 15 after forty-two days on the trail. The fortuitous survival of Bell's diary preserved a chronicle of this nearly forgotten era of cattle drives that crossed the Pecos many miles below the fabled drive at Horsehead.

The Highest Bridge

Before railroads reached the Pecos, the military built spindly pontoon bridges to help move troops and supplies. None was made to last. The railroad bridges became the first with any degree of permanence to span the river.

By 1881, three railroads were working to forge a steel route across Texas. The Texas and Pacific Railway was moving southwestward from Fort Worth. The Southern Pacific began laying track east from El Paso, racing the westbound Texas and Pacific. A few months earlier, the Galveston, Harrisburg and San Antonio Railroad had started construction westward from San Antonio. The latter faced the greatest challenge, crossing the Pecos River canyon, three hundred feet deep and two thousand feet across.

Deciding that the canyon was too wide to cross, the engineers mapped a winding route that descended to the Rio Grande. They carved a narrow right of way along the river's cliffs to the Pecos, which was bridged with a standard wooden one slightly above the water line. The tracks then climbed gradually out of the canyon on the western side. This route required additional bridges across several canyons entering the Rio Grande and two large tunnels blasted through solid rock. When completed, trains slowly navigated the tortuous twelve-mile Loop Line. Sections of grade below a narrow ledge cut from the cliff walls required "track-walkers" to constantly check for rock falls blocking the track.

Almost immediately, plans began for a viaduct bridge across the Pecos. A spot was chosen some five miles upriver. The Phoenix Bridge Company of Phoenixville, Pennsylvania, contracted to build the iron bridge, which would sit atop concrete and limestone pillars. The company, organized in 1864, had constructed more than eight hundred bridges, many of them for railroads.

Work began on November 3, 1891. The bridge was completed in only 103 days. Prebuilt sections of the bridge were assembled on both sides of the river. Once the pillars were in place, a bridge section was moved by a machine called a "traveler" to carry the bridge section and lower it in place.

Traveling crane adding bridge piece on west side of Pecos River. *Special Collections, Lehigh University Libraries, Bethlehem, Pennsylvania.*

Construction began on the east side of the Pecos. When the center of the bridge was reached, the traveler was dismantled, shipped by rail to the west side and reassembled to complete the bridge. The work was highly dangerous, and several men died during the construction. Judge Roy Bean was called from Langtry for the inquests. In one incident, seven men were killed, and three others mortally injured. Bean, not wanting to make two trips, pronounced all ten dead.

On March 31, 1892, a special train carrying railroad dignitaries officially opened the Pecos Viaduct to regular rail traffic. The completed bridge was 2,180 feet long and 321 feet high and consisted of 1,820 tons of ironwork. When constructed, it was the highest railroad bridge in North America and the third highest in the world. For many years, trains would pause and slowly cross the bridge to allow passengers time to enjoy the spectacular view of the bridge and the canyon.

Within twenty years, increasing traffic and heavier loads were straining the viaduct's abilities. In 1929, structural changes were made to increase the load capacity of the bridge.

With the coming of World War II, the strategic significance of this line, the fastest route between Houston and San Francisco, led to placing troops at the bridge to secure it from sabotage. Realizing that the aging viaduct

Pecos River as seen from High Bridge, near LANGTRY, Texas.

Old postcard view of the Lower Pecos country. *Author's collection.*

Pecos High Bridge nearing completion with the viaduct in background. *Archives of the Big Bend.*

might be unable to handle the increased war traffic, a new bridge was begun in August 1943.

The new bridge was built 440 feet downstream from the viaduct, where the canyon had stable walls some 770 feet apart, with a depth of 322 feet to the water level. The bridge was a continuous cantilever type set atop two unusually tall concrete piers. One of them stands 275 feet high from its rock foundation. Planned for far heavier loads, the structure was also designed to handle high winds and earthquakes. The $1.2 million bridge used the least amount of steelwork (2,700 tons), a wartime necessity.

The Pecos High Bridge opened to main line traffic on December 21, 1994, and has remained in operation to the present day. The old viaduct continued as a standby until 1949, when the Southern Pacific contracted to dismantle it. Various tales exist regarding its fate. One claimed that it was sold to Guatemala and still in operation in the late 1970s. Another placed it on the Wabash River in Indiana. The truth was less impressive. Individual bridge spans were sold to states and local governments for shorter bridges, and the remaining pieces were purchased by scrap metal dealers.

THE NORTHERN ROUTE

No towering cliffs blocked the construction of a northern railroad to the Pecos, but the landscape through which it ran held its own formidable challenges. The region between the edge of the Mescalero Escarpment of the Llano Estacado and the Pecos River contains a vast sheet of sand. The sandhills were created from ancient portions of the Rocky Mountains, eroded by the Pecos River over forty thousand years ago, and then blown into an expanse of sand dunes and thin sandy topsoil. Sometimes, in areas of harder subsoil, pools of water temporarily form, but otherwise there is no surface water besides the river. For early travelers attempting to cross the region, it was a significant barrier. Today, the drive across the sands remains desolate.

The region proved especially dangerous for a crew of surveyors mapping the future Texas and Pacific Railway route in 1880. Major R.J. Lawrence and his men almost perished in the sandhills when they exhausted their water supply. As men and animals began suffering from thirst, they abandoned wagons along forty miles of the trail. Crazed with thirst, some men stripped off their clothes as they struggled westward to reach the Pecos.

The Sandhills east of the Pecos. *Photograph by author.*

A few hardier souls finally reached the river and returned in search of stragglers. Several, blinded by the white sands, plunged in headfirst upon reaching the river. Three others were found drinking the blood of an animal they had killed. Although livestock was lost, all the crew survived the trek. The survey through the sandhills was temporarily abandoned until men and animals recovered.

The T&P railroad construction crews had no problem navigating this bleak region bordering the Pecos, but they did struggle with the problem of water. Water for operating trains had to be shipped from the "midway" point (present-day Midland) ninety miles to the east until a well at Monyhans (present-day Monahans) was completed. The construction crew of two hundred men and forty mule teams averaged laying a mile and a half of track per day across the relatively flat terrain. Bridging the Pecos proved no great challenge. The newspaper correspondent simply remarked that the tracks crossed the river on July 23, commenting that it was "bank full and very muddy and runs swift."

He reserved harsher descriptions for the terrain: "The country west of the Sand Hills is a barren waste of alkali soil, not fit for fish, flesh, or fowl, worse than the Dry Tortugas, a regular Gehenna, more lonesome than the Arctic circle, hotter than the equator, dryer than a powder horn."

The completed railroad line faced troubles in the sandhills. Sandstorms often blew out holes in the roadbed, delaying trains. It was also not uncommon for a belligerent buffalo astride the tracks to halt trains.

Automobile travel discovered its own problems crossing the region. In the years just prior to World War I, West Texans advocated for a transcontinental highway across Texas beside the path of the Texas and Pacific route. Following the passage of the national Federal Aid Road Act of 1916, popularly known as the Bankhead Bill after its primary sponsor, Texas created a highway commission the following year. When the Texas Highway Commission drew up the first plans for a Texas highway system, the road was designated Texas Highway No. 1 as part of the national Bankhead Highway.

The first automobile group to attempt to drive the proposed Bankhead route encountered an unusual problem: too much water. The Second Army Transcontinental Motor Convoy set out from Washington in June 1920. Rain and poor roads caused the convoy to arrive in Texarkana in August, a week behind schedule. Exceptional West Texas rainfall continued as they journeyed westward, frequently bogging the heavy trucks in the poor Texas roads. The monthly average sometimes reached as much as that in a normal year.

Finally, at Sweetwater, the convoy abandoned the Bankhead path, turning south to San Angelo. From there, they followed the Texas and Orient Railway route. Returning north at the Pecos River, the convoy crossed the river at Grand Falls and rejoined the Bankhead route near Pyote. From there, they completed a much drier journey to El Paso.

By 1922, much of the Bankhead, redesignated as U.S. Highway 80, was under construction. It required a decade to pave the entire Texas stretch. A 1925 highway report described the road as "graded and graveled" from Sweetwater to Odessa and "rough and rocky from Monahans to Kent" with plenty of detours around road work. For a time, the unpaved Highway 80 across Texas was sarcastically referred to as "Ma Ferguson's Dirt Road," named for the first woman governor of Texas.

Modern travelers on Interstate 20 streaking across the Pecos River at eighty miles per hour pay little attention to the river or the arid terrain. They have no idea of the trials encountered while building routes across this "Gehenna."

The Last Bridge

For years, you encountered them on almost any Texas drive, their steel frame flashing by as you crossed a river. The metal Parker Truss bridges were once a common Texas highway fixture. One of the primary bridge types built between 1905 and 1940, they provided quick and safe passage over rivers and waterways across the state. The arching top chord of these bridges led to the nickname of "Camelback trusses." The sawtooth pattern of the steel created a delicate-looking yet highly sturdy passage.

Today, these old veterans of highway travel are becoming increasingly rare sights. Some have been transplanted to reside in parks, on hike-and-bike trails or along access routes. Others stand abandoned. The one spanning the Pecos River on State Highway 290 may be among the last few remaining in active service.

In the early twentieth century, automobiles were a rare novelty in West Texas. Dirt roads mostly served wagon travel. Railroads remained the principal means for long-distance journeys. Without bridges, the Pecos proved an almost impassable obstacle for cars. In 1906, Pecos County built a small bridge across the river near the crossing on the old stage and wagon trail from San Antonio for $8,000, and the first motorists drove into western Crockett County.

Before World War I, a group of entrepreneurs from several southern states worked for the development of a transcontinental road. The Old Spanish Trail Association (OST) envisioned linking communities across the South and West from San Augustine, Florida, to San Diego, California. Nine hundred miles of that route, almost one third, were in Texas.

The Federal Aid Road Act and the creation of the Texas Highway Commission greatly aided their cause. Under the leadership of Harral Ayres, the OST worked with towns and counties to construct its route across Texas. The OST even developed its own distinctive signage, using red, white and yellow markings (the Spanish flag's colors), and including route designations and even turn guidance. Communities all along the route were encouraged to promote local history and culture in an early version of heritage tourism.

The Old Spanish Trail Highway gradually became a reality in the 1920s as more motorists set out on journeys long and short. By 1929, Ayres and the OST had pronounced the road finished. The reality fell short of ideal. Many long miles on each side of the Pecos were still listed as gravel, "improved dirt" or just plain "dirt." Taking paths of least resistance and easiest grade, roads navigated hills using switchback turns and wandered long miles alongside rivers and creeks. Westbound drivers avoided the steep old military road at Lancaster Hill, descending to Live Oak Creek several miles upstream from the mouth. Following the creek downstream, they turned west near the ruins of Fort Lancaster to reach the county bridge across the Pecos.

In the 1930s, despite the Depression, highway construction continued across the state. Highways now bore number designations and standardized signage. The OST path through West Texas became State Highway 27. Roads were straightened and shortened, and sturdier bridges of steel and concrete added.

A new asphalt road with deep mountain cuts and stone walls bordering the edge curved down Lancaster Hill across from the old wagon road built in 1849. Drivers stopping at the new rest stop before descending the winding grade could trace the diagonal path down to the old fort ruins visible below.

In 1932, M.H. Ryland contracted with the Texas Highway Department to build a new Pecos River bridge a few miles downstream from the

View of old wagon road down Lancaster Hill from the Highway 290 roadside park. *Photograph by author.*

The Texas Highway 290 Pecos River bridge. *Courtesy of James Michael Collett.*

county one. It would be a sturdy steel Parker Truss–type bridge capable of a longer span across the Pecos. Beginning on the eastern side of the river, a 607-foot causeway crossed the floodplain; 152 feet of concrete and steel spanned the river 30 feet above the waterline. An additional 295-foot concrete causeway connected the west bank. The bridge stood at the southeastern boundary of my great-grandfather Smith's ranch.

The new two-lane asphalt highway was opened to traffic later that same year. State Highway 27 eventually became part of U.S. Highway 290. For the next fifty years, a steadily growing stream of automobiles and trucks rolled across that bridge, carrying an immense volume of tourists and truckers. For me, meeting a line of eighteen-wheelers on that bridge was always a white-knuckle experience!

In the early 1980s, completion of one of the last segments of Interstate 10 sliced deep cuts across the Edwards Plateau and crossed the river five miles upstream. By then, the old Parker Truss style of bridge was no longer used. The new Pecos River bridges were hardly noticeable.

Demoted to state highway status, the 1930s highway across the Edwards Plateau to an intersection eight miles west of the Pecos remains an active road. The traffic is sparse, mostly local. The old bridge shows its age, its silver paint peeling in many places, the beams rusted, the concrete weathered. Yet it still sturdily spans the Pecos as a reminder of days when highway trips were more of an adventure along less direct paths. For those with the time or inclination to leave the interstate for a while, Highway 290 provides a great nostalgic ride of yesteryear travel, including a crossing of the Pecos on one of the last classic Parker Truss Texas highway bridges.

CONTESTED WATERS

The mortuary shelter contained the cremated remains of three Native Americans, a male, a female and an adolescent, probably male. The lack of habitation, the skull of an eagle and the impressive view northeast toward the Pecos all implied some special status of the dead. Skeletal analysis pointed to the conclusion that the three, perhaps a family, met a violent end sometime around eight hundred years ago. Violence done to these, and other, ancient bones discovered in the Pecos River Country establish that conflict among different peoples has existed here for centuries, although the details of those clashes are lost in time. As Spanish and later Anglo-American people entered this region, violent confrontations became more common.

THE GREAT ROCK

Captain Juan Dominguez de Mendoza arrived at the Jumano village of Jediondos on the Pecos River on January 17, 1684. He halted his party of soldiers, missionaries and Indian allies a league from the village. The Natives were expecting them. A large party—some on foot, others on horseback—met the Spaniards. Their leader, Juan Sabeata, fired an old arquebus, with others also firing weapons. Captain Dominguez ordered his soldiers to fire two volleys in response.

This was friendly gunfire, however. The Spanish came at the request of Jumano leaders, including Sabeata. Sabeata, a baptized Christian convert, had traveled to El Paso requesting Spanish help against the raids by hostile Apache bands. He also appealed for missionaries, claiming that he had a miraculous vision of a holy cross above his village.

The nomadic hunter-gatherer Jumano ranged across much of western Texas, hunting buffalo and trading with various groups. They lived along the Pecos River but wandered eastward to the Concho Rivers and south to the La Junta region, where the Rio Conchos of Mexico meets the Rio Grande (near present-day Presidio). Receptive to Spanish influence, they served as middlemen between the Spanish colonies and other Indian tribes.

The Jediondos villagers carried a weathered, six-foot wooden cross, painted red and yellow, and a two-foot white cloth banner, decorated with blue crosses. Mendoza halted his soldiers until the priests dismounted to kneel before the cross, as did he. Some Indians kissed the hem of the priests' robes.

The Spaniards followed the Natives to the village. Jediondos spanned both sides of the river, on the east bank of which stood a steep butte that sat apart from the tier of mesas forming the eastern wall of the river valley. In his journal, Mendoza describes it as "a great rock," which the Jumanos said

The "Great Rock" of the Jumano. *Photograph by author.*

45

protected them from the Apache. Mendoza established his camp nearby, naming it San Ygnacio de Loyola.

After spending a week among the Jumano and promising to make war against the Apache, Mendoza continued eastward in search of pearls (in the Concho rivers) and to establish a mission and bastion (possibly on the San Saba River). Several thousand friendly Indians camped around them. After three fierce attacks by the Apache, Mendoza abandoned the mission six weeks later, planning to return with more force. However, Spanish concerns about rumors of the French venturing into East Texas ended Mendoza's plans for a West Texas mission.

On an archaeological field trip several years ago, we climbed Mendoza's "great rock" beside the Pecos. The butte proved a difficult ascent. With an impassible limestone outcrop capping the western side, we scrambled up the steep eastern slope across a loose talus of rock.

The summit provided a dramatic panorama of the Pecos River Valley for miles. The river curved beneath the base of the mesa 180 feet below, where a freshwater spring once flowed. Anyone approaching could be seen miles away. Standing atop this "great rock," I realized that it occupied a particularly significant geographical spot. Like some prehistoric Gibraltar, it marks where the Pecos River leaves the flat, open terrain it has wandered across to enter a valley bordered by limestone mesas and walls, which become increasingly steep and narrow near the Rio Grande.

As we walked the narrow spine of the mountaintop, we found three distinct stone circles in a rough north–south alignment along the ridge. Two were little more than jumbled stone circles nine feet in diameter, scattered rocks indicating once taller walls. Gaps implied south-facing entrances. The more impressive northernmost circle consisted of two and three courses of stacked stone, varying in size and shape, with one large stone standing on end. There was a scatter of ashy soil and burned rock.

North of these structures, the mesa topsoil thinned, becoming solid, gray limestone rock. Two irregular rock piles formed small, mounded cairns, loosely assembled, holding nothing but stone.

Had the Jumanos built these dwellings, bases for wickiups finished with sotol stalks and a cover of brush or hides, as sentinel points to watch for approaching danger? Did the "great rock" become a citadel from which to hurl down destruction on any who dared to attack? Or did others build these high outposts?

Former state archaeologist Robert Mallouf studied similar structures in the La Junta region and beyond for years. Naming them the Cielo Complex

Stone circle atop butte on the Pecos River. *Photograph by author.*

(the Spanish word for "sky"), he found that they were almost invariably built on well-elevated, strategically located landforms—small buttes, promontories, ridges—with extensive views of the surrounding terrain. The scattered debitage and arrow points found with them indicated that their builders constructed them in the late Prehistoric period, just before historic records began with the Spanish arrival. That they were defensive positions is certainly one obvious conclusion.

Are those great rocks atop the butte beside the Pecos the last remaining trace of Jediondos? Perhaps. Perhaps not. We will most likely never definitively know. Yet I like to imagine standing there with the great encampment of Jumanos on the river below as the scouts spy the first flashes of sunlight from the armor of the approaching Spanish expedition.

THE FLAGPOLE FIGHT

That October 1855 morning, Captain Stephen Carpenter set out with a small detail up Live Oak Creek in search of a tree—narrow and straight—

to serve as a flagpole for the military post he and his infantry troops had established a few months earlier, just above where the creek met the Pecos River. Carpenter rode his favorite horse, Driver, his two hunting dogs trotting beside him. On the trip to the live oak grove, he also planned to hunt for turkeys along the creek. He had no idea how deadly this little expedition would become.

Captain Stephen Decatur Carpenter commanded Company H of the First U.S. Infantry. Less than two months earlier, on August 20, 1855, he led Companies H and K from Fort Duncan on the Rio Grande to Camp Lancaster on Live Oak Creek, a half mile above its confluence with the Pecos River. The post would help protect the Lower Route to California.

Carpenter was a career officer, having served in the army since his 1840 West Point graduation. He had fought in two conflicts, the Second Seminole and Mexican-American Wars, and participated in the construction and garrisoning of several Texas frontier posts.

Jacob Stillman, a civilian doctor contracted to serve the post, accompanied the group. Stillman, long fascinated with the Lone Star State, embarked on a journey in 1855 to study its natural history. On this October 12 day, he found more than enough adventure.

Carpenter's party included three soldiers, a teamster and a six-mule wagon team. The group traveled slowly up the creek as the narrow stream was often congested with small trees, underbrush and grapevines. About a mile above where the stage trail curved back to the east, toward a climb up the Edwards Plateau, they reached a large grove, and the men set to work.

Carpenter and Stillman rode off in search of turkeys, soon losing sight of each other in the brush. Stillman heard a pistol shot. Assuming that Carpenter had found some game, he headed toward the sound and crossed a trail marking the recent passage of several horses. He found the captain and his dogs returning through brush. Carpenter had indeed found and wounded a turkey. As he and the dogs trailed it over a ridge, he saw a party of Indians, most likely Apaches, on the opposite slope. He estimated the group to be around nineteen well-mounted warriors, armed with shields, bows and arrows, lances and a few guns. Uncertain if he had been seen or heard, he returned to his group, ordering them to quickly complete their work, while he watched the Indians from the trees.

With the long flagstaff finally cut and loaded, the party started back, lumbering through the thick brush, Carpenter in the lead. While he paused for his horse to forage, Stillman heard a fierce yell. He saw the teamster fleeing from two warriors who overtook and struck him down. Joined by a

Live Oak Creek, site of the flagpole fight. *Photograph by author.*

third, the Indians charged Stillman "like bloodhounds, without a sound." He fled for the fort in terror. Exhausted, he dashed into camp, certain that Captain Carpenter was dead.

Carpenter had been with the wagons when the warriors broke from the woods, splitting to encircle the party. They intended to stampede the animals, run down the men and kill them all. Carpenter and the troopers dismounted. He ordered the men not to fire until the Indians drew close enough to make their shots effective.

Thwarted in their stampede plans, the Indians used the brush as cover as they worked closer to the soldiers. They would appear, loose an arrow and quickly duck out of sight, yelling fiercely. When the enemy was within fifty yards, the soldiers returned fire.

Two warriors, blowing whistles to signal or encourage the assault, advanced on Carpenter from different sides, firing from behind their shields. The captain held Driver's reins and his shotgun with his left hand. He swept the revolver in his right hand back and forth between the two Indians. His shots had little effect. The warriors, now within a dozen paces, were more successful. An arrow struck Driver in the neck, causing him to rear in pain and terror. Arrows pierced the captain's clothing, and one stuck in his boot. Another struck his right hand, his pistol stopping it from passing through into his body.

Determined to die fighting, Carpenter leveled his pistol at one warrior. When he raised his shield, Carpenter quickly fired at the second one, catching him unprepared. The bullet struck the Indian in the chest, killing him. Dropping his empty pistol, Carpenter turned desperately to raise the shotgun against the other warrior. Fortunately, a shot from one of the troopers cut down the Indian seconds before he reached the wounded officer.

Stillman had climbed the ridge behind the new post to look for survivors. He was startled but elated to see the captain riding in slowly, the dogs crimson and Driver rapidly losing blood. When the doctor started to dress Carpenter's wounded hand, the captain ordered him to first do what he could for his horse.

A stronger force returned to the battlefield the following day to recover the body of the teamster, the wagon and team and the flagpole. They found no other bodies. The Indians had removed them.

DEADLY PASSAGE

The blazing of the Goodnight-Loving Cattle Trail in 1866 created a steady flow of cattle westward to Horsehead Crossing on the Pecos River. Many drives reaching the difficult crossing found themselves facing additional danger. The Comanches had long used the crossing on their forays into Mexico for horses and captives. They quickly seized this opportunity to steal cattle from unwary cattlemen and drive them into New Mexico to trade with comancheros. Many drives lost cattle, horses and sometimes lives in confrontations with the deadly warriors. Even Charles Goodnight, who always took extra precautions, observed Indians delivering stock he lost at Horsehead to Fort Sumner, New Mexico.

Perhaps the worst disaster to befall a cattleman encountering the fierce Comanches at Horsehead was that of Andy M. Adams in 1867. Adams secured a lucrative beef contract with Fort Sumner. To fill it, four herds from Llano and the headwaters of the Concho River set out in the spring of that year.

George Hepburn, with nine drovers, led the first herd of 656 animals on the trail on April 17. They reached the Pecos on the night of the twenty-fifth, where a large party of Comanches drove off over half the herd. The next morning, Hepburn and some of the crew recovered 38 head, but the raiders returned that night, stealing 15 horses.

A second group of Adams's cattle, divided into three closely separated herds, totaling over 2,000 head, headed west on May 4. Just two days on the trail, two of the herds were attacked by a party of 150 to 300 Indians, perhaps Kickapoos. One drover was captured and skinned alive. Other cowboys escaped into a thicket. The remainder fought from behind their wagons and oxen, finally escaping at daylight. The cattle were lost. The following night, the raiders struck the third group, capturing their livestock. The drovers recovered 103 the next day, less than a fourth of the almost 500 with which they started.

The next herd fared even worse. Led by Joey Hoy with eleven drovers, they left Spring Creek on May 15 with 250 head of cattle. Hoy brought his wife and four children, believing that they would be safer than if left at home. He could not have been more wrong.

Approaching Horsehead, the cattle, starved for water, dashed to the river. Catching up, the party prepared to eat when they saw a cloud of dust. The Indian band soon arrived and began driving horses and cattle away. Hoy maneuvered the wagon with the children into a ravine to hide as the group prepared for a fight. Mrs. Hoy helped load guns for the men as they fired into the attacking warriors, who were armed with both guns and bows and arrows. The besieged managed to kill an Indian, his body quickly carried away by his companions. Several of the cowhands were wounded, including Mrs. Hoy, who was shot in the hip.

When their attackers withdrew to round up the cattle, the party gathered what few horses they could and retreated to the adobe ruins of a Butterfield stage stand. They huddled there for three days, while the Indians burned their other wagons and supplies. On the fourth day, a band of gold hunters arrived and rescued the party. Hoy never recovered any money for the lost cattle.

Adams's final herd left Llano on May 15 with Orville Oatman in charge. They lost 135 head in a stampede before even reaching Horsehead with the remaining 800. A large war party of Comanches and Kiowas attacked, seizing the herd, along with fifteen horses and mules. Taking refuge in a sinkhole, the drovers survived a siege of several days with only two wounded.

This deadly season of depredation at the crossing finally ended with the reoccupation of Fort Stockton by the U.S. Army later that year.

A Dubious Distinction

Fort Lancaster has the dubious distinction of being the only U.S. Army post in Texas to be attacked by Native Americans. That small battle, however, also earned a significant spot in the Reconstruction-era history of the Buffalo Soldiers.

Federal troops abandoned Fort Lancaster with the outbreak of the Civil War. For several months, Confederate forces occupied the fort until the spring of 1862, when it was abandoned for the remainder of the war, unprotected from decay and damage by Native American groups.

Following the war's end, federal troops returned to Texas. Many consisted of Black soldiers under the command of white officers. Lancaster served as a sub-post for Fort Stockton, which was occupied by the Ninth Cavalry, a Black cavalry regiment, in 1867. Company K, commanded by Captain William Frohock, was assigned to Lancaster.

The troops stayed busy restoring fort buildings and providing escort to stages on San Antonio–El Paso line, which had a relay station at the old fort. Three troopers died on escort duty in skirmishes with Apaches. Otherwise, things were relatively quiet at the post. Until the day after Christmas.

On the afternoon of December 26, 1867, routine duties were underway. A mounted detail was driving the company's horses and mules from the pasture to water at the creek. Another group drove a wagon to the creek to fill water barrels and gather firewood. Everything seemed a leisurely, post-Christmas day.

Using the creek as cover, two large group of Kickapoos approached from the north. The Kickapoos had relocated to Mexico, following their success repulsing an attack at Dove Creek in 1865. From there, they conducted raids into Texas. Joining the Kickapoos were Mexicans and renegade white attackers. One of the war parties passed downstream unseen, positioning to attack. The second closed on the wagon detail.

Private William Sharpe, with the wagon, saw the group approaching along the creek and warned the others of the impending attack. The wagon detail ran for cover, but Sharpe was overrun and killed.

Two hundred mounted Kickapoos charged the horse escort from the north. The horse guard fought to turn the herd back toward the corral as they fired into the attacking force. Two of the soldiers, Privates Eli Bower and Anderson Trimble, were dragged from their horses and killed. A second group attacked from the west, preventing access to the corral. As the troopers frantically took shelter in buildings or formed skirmish lines and began firing their Spencer carbines, the large body of warriors to the south joined the assault. The post was now under assault on three fronts by more than four hundred attackers.

The soldiers were unable to get the fear-crazed horses into the corral, and they stampeded into the southern assault. Fortunately for the troopers, the Kickapoos turned their attention to capturing the horses. Otherwise, Captain Frohock wrote in his report, "It is doubtful if the defense against such overwhelming odds could have been successful." The Kickapoos withdrew out of range of the carbines with their captured herd.

Captain Frohock led most of the company to attempt to recapture the horses, but the Kickapoos remained beyond the effective range of the carbines, keeping the horses behind them. When the force to the north launched another attack, Frohock ordered his troops back to the thinly defended fort. Steady gunfire eventually drove this group away.

Company K prepared for a deadly fight on multiple fronts with a force Captain Frohock now estimated as large as nine hundred. However, having captured the horse herd, the attackers appeared satisfied. Making no further assaults, the warriors moved on after dark with their stolen mounts, thirty-eight horses and six mules.

Ruins of Fort Lancaster around 1900. Photograph by J. Stokley Ligon. *Archives of the Big Bend.*

At daylight, the troopers searched for the bodies of the three dead soldiers. They would not recover the bodies for several months. They found two dead Indians and estimated that they may have killed as many as twenty and wounded more. The soldiers collected items scattered over the battleground—bows, quivers of arrows, a Remington revolver and a headdress with twenty silver plates.

Two days later, a raiding party returned and attempted to capture the few mounts remaining at the fort but were unsuccessful. They headed down the Pecos, and the Battle of Fort Lancaster was over.

The fight at Fort Lancaster was the first major battle fought by the Ninth Cavalry. Their courage under fire against overwhelming odds clearly established their credentials as a frontier fighting force. The African American frontier regiments would earn the nickname of "Buffalo Soldiers," given them by the Natives they fought because their dark, curly hair resembled a buffalo's coat but also because of their fierce fighting ability. Company K of the Ninth earned part of that reputation at Fort Lancaster.

"DON'T LET US LEAVE HIM"

As he spurred his horse to escape the pursuing warriors, Sergeant Ward realized that the lieutenant was not with them. Had he escaped in a different direction? Or was he still behind, directly in the path of the charging Indians? Was there time to locate and rescue him? Ward had only seconds to decide.

The Black Seminole Indian Scouts were created in 1870, under the command of Lieutenant John L. Bullis to serve on the Texas frontier during the Indian Wars. They were descendants of slaves who escaped to Florida, then under Spanish rule, and assimilated with Seminole people living there. After the United States acquired Florida, the Black Seminoles were among those forcibly moved west to Indian Territory.

In addition to other hardships, they faced the threat of kidnapping and being returned to slavery. In 1850, a group of the Black Seminoles moved to Mexico to be free of the re-enslavement danger. The Mexican government welcomed and enlisted their help in fighting the Comanche and Apache raiding parties into Mexico.

Twenty years later, they sought to return to the United States. Major Zenas Bliss of the Twenty-Fifth Infantry, one of the Buffalo Soldier units, offered the Black Seminoles positions as scouts. In July 1870, a group arrived at

Black Seminole Indian Scouts. *Public domain.*

Fort Duncan to become scouts. In August, the U.S. Army created the Black Seminole Indian Scouts. From 1873 until 1881, Lieutenant John Lapham Bullis led the scouts.

Unorthodox, the scouts proved themselves exceptional trackers and fighters. They often dressed in non-military clothing, even like Indians at times. They spoke English and border Spanish and sometimes prayed in Seminole. They participated in military operations of all sizes, from patrols to major campaigns. One of their most dangerous encounters occurred not far from the Pecos River.

On April 25, 1875, Bullis and three scouts—Sergeant John Ward, Private Pompey Factor and trumpeter Isaac Payne—discovered a fresh trail of seventy-five horses stolen by Indians and followed it toward the Pecos River. At Eagle's Nest Crossing, they caught up with the raiding party of thirty warriors as they were preparing to drive the horses across the Rio Grande.

Tethering their horses, the soldiers crept within seventy-five yards of the Indians and then opened fire. In a gun battle over the next forty-five minutes, they killed three Indians and wounded a fourth. Twice, the scouts were able to drive off the stolen horses, only to lose them again. The Indians, armed with Winchester repeaters, had the greater firepower. Realizing the small size of the force attacking them, the warriors attempted to cut the soldiers off from their horses.

The four men ran for their horses to escape. The Seminoles mounted and were speeding away when they realized that Lieutenant Bullis was not with them. Looking back, they saw he was unable to mount his frightened horse and remained afoot in the path of the charging warriors.

Sergeant Ward shouted to the others, "Boys, don't let us leave him." He turned his horse around, followed by his fellow troopers. Seeing their maneuver, the Indians directed heavy gunfire toward the approaching men. As Ward reached the lieutenant, a bullet sliced through his carbine sling.

While Ward pulled Bullis behind him on his horse, a second shot shattered the stock of his carbine. As the two fled just ahead of the Natives, Factor and Pompey shot into the charging warriors. Their heavy fire brought down four of them, causing the rest to check their pursuit. The four soldiers made the fifty-six-mile journey back to Fort Clark without stopping. Bullis later reported that the three scouts "saved my hair."

For their heroic rescue, Ward, Factor and Payne received the Congressional Medal of Honor on May 28, 1875. Bullis and his scouts continued campaigns against hostiles along the border, sometimes pursuing them across the Rio Grande, in twenty-five expeditions over eight years. In many of their actions, they were heavily outnumbered, but the scouts never lost a man wounded or killed in action.

POST ON THE PECOS

Fort Lancaster was one of the most isolated posts in Texas. Companies H and K of the U.S. First Infantry occupied the post for most of its life. Federal troops evacuated the post in early 1861. During the Civil War, Texan and Confederate troops attempted to man the frontier forts, but the effort was soon abandoned. Following the war, Lancaster served as a sub-post for the Ninth Cavalry regiment. It was permanently abandoned in the late 1870s. Beyond the official post returns and documents, other surviving records provide more personal glimpses into the lives of some for whom it was home.

THE CAPTAIN'S CAMEL RIDE

As federal troops spread across the West in the 1850s, the issue of supplying them remained a constant challenge. Secretary of War Jefferson Davis became a prominent supporter of an unusual option: camels. Funding was finally secured in 1855, and camels were imported from North Africa and the Middle East over the next two years. Major Henry Wayne, who oversaw the importation, transported the camels and their Arab caretakers to Camp Verde, Texas, the headquarters for the camel experiment.

Former navy man Edward Fitzgerald Beale, long an advocate for the use of camels on the frontier, became the first to try the animals in the field.

Fort Lancaster State Historic Site. *Photograph by author.*

Twenty-five camels were field-tested as a pack train in the laying out of a wagon road from Fort Defiance, Arizona, to the Colorado River. Nineteen-year-old May Humphreys Stacey accompanied this expedition, serving as a chronicler.

On June 25, 1857, forty men, forty-six mules and seven horses, wagons, dogs and twenty-five camels, each with a pack weighing 576 pounds, set out westward from Camp Verde. They traveled along the San Antonio–El Paso Road and across the rugged Trans-Pecos with phenomenal endurance. Their padded feet proved exceptionally suited to the rough, jagged terrain. Their resistance to the arid country surpassed that of any other pack animal. They adapted well to surviving on the scarce forage of the land, eating screwbean, greasewood and mesquite brush. With the camels averaging twenty miles per day, Beale became increasingly fond of them. "The more I see of them the more interested in them I become," he wrote, "and the more I am convinced of their usefulness." He wished he had twice as many.

The party reached the edge of the Edwards Plateau above Fort Lancaster on the morning of July 9. Descending the steep road, they camped on Live Oak Creek two miles from the fort. After a day spent repairing saddles and doctoring wounds on the camels' backs, Beale and several of the party visited the fort to attend the funeral of infant Arthur Lee.

When they arrived at the fort, the camels became the center of attention, the entire post turning out to see them. Captain Stephen Carpenter was invited to take a ride on one, to which he readily agreed. After dismounting, the captain commented that, after getting used to the motion, he would prefer a camel to a mule.

Following the funeral, Carpenter invited Beale, Stacey and the others to dine with him. Tired of the "salt junk and hard biscuit" of the trail, they quickly accepted. The meal was an excellent one, especially given the remote location of the post. Claret was served with ham, eggs, rolls and butter. Dessert consisted of preserved peaches, with cream and fruit cake. Stacey wrote, "I can say I never tasted better in my life." Carpenter's wife, Laura, served as hostess for the meal, her conversation prompting Stacey to comment that she was "one of the cleverest little women we have seen in Texas."

After dining, the men followed the expedition's wagons, which had already departed for the Pecos. Stacey recorded no difficulties with the Pecos, and Beale's expedition continued across West Texas and beyond. At Albuquerque, the camels were loaded with seven hundred pounds each for the trip to Colorado and fared better with less water than the horses and mules.

In subsequent years, Lieutenant Edward Hartz and Lieutenant William Echols conducted successful camel trials in the Trans-Pecos. The camel experiment, however, fell victim to the coming of the Civil War, preventing any real application. Most of the camels were released into the countryside, where for many years an occasional wanderer might encounter one of the beasts, to the astonishment of both.

And Captain Carpenter, a career soldier who had already served in two wars and fought a battle with Lipan a few miles from the fort, added this experience to his adventures.

The Captain's Wife

On a Friday evening in February 1858, Laura Carpenter sat down to write her husband a letter. Captain Stephen Carpenter had recently departed for court-martial duty in San Antonio. This was their first separation since their marriage in October 1856. The evening was quiet at Fort Lancaster. The officers' quarters were warm from the fireplace, the plastered adobe walls glowing in the lantern light.

Laura wrote, "My own Darling, I have nothing to tell but thought twould be a little bit like seeing you tonight to write the words which your dear eyes may look upon a week or two hence." She assured him, "I have not had a bad spell of coughing since you left." He should have no concerns about home. She had friends dropping by, and his ten-year-old daughter, Alice, had been "very good." The evening quiet made her drowsy, so "with warm embraces and sweet goodnight kisses," she closed her letter. "I write myself, for the first time, your own true loving wife."

A long journey had brought Laura to the far West Texas frontier with her officer husband. Laura Clark was born in Hampden, Maine, in 1825. In 1851, at twenty-six years old, she journeyed by ship to Brazoria, Texas, to work as a "schoolmarm" on a large plantation. She hoped that a more southern climate would improve her health, damaged by a consumption-like illness.

Thomas Pilsbury owned the plantation. He had migrated to Texas from Maine years before with his wife, Rebecca, and became influential in Texas politics. Laura found the job teaching planters' sons and daughters pleasant, with "not a stupid one among them." The Pilsburys invited her to social events, including cotillions.

Perhaps there, in the Pilsbury household, she met Rebecca's brother, a dark-haired army captain. A widower, Carpenter had lost his wife in childbirth in 1852. The couple's first child, Alice, was now eight.

The two found much in common. Carpenter was himself a Maine native, born in Paris, ninety miles from Hampden. A romance blossomed, followed by marriage, and Laura became an army wife. She followed him to his assigned post, Fort Lancaster. Arriving at the top of Lancaster Hill, where the wagon wheels were chained to descend the steep road to the fort, Laura knew that she was a long distance from Maine. Another army wife described the fort as "the worst of all posts in Texas."

For Laura, however, it was now home, with the man she had chosen to marry and follow wherever that led. Her intelligence and positive demeanor helped her make friends at the post and impress guests the captain invited to their limestone and adobe officer's quarters. She worked to replace the mother Alice had lost.

Laura had followed her heart to a life on the Texas frontier. The arid climate perhaps helped her cough, but the constant dust probably offset the benefits. Laura added a note to her letter, requesting ginger for her cough and twenty yards of stout cloth for sewing projects. Then she encouraged her husband: "When you get started for home you must make long marches." Captain Carpenter returned to the fort on March 2.

In April 1859, Laura accompanied Stephen back east, possibly to take Alice to stay with family in Maine. A new assignment awaited the captain upon their return. Carpenter was to take Company H west to Comanche Springs to make Camp Stockton a permanent fort.

Laura followed her husband to Camp Stockton in October that year. Life there was far more primitive. The couple resided in an adobe house roofed with thatch, supposedly "fit for occupation." This pre–Civil War post was replaced after the war by one farther to the east. Any remains of it now lie beneath the streets of Fort Stockton.

The following year, Laura became pregnant. John Carpenter was born in the fall of 1860. The strains of frontier life, childbirth and poor health proved too much. Laura died on November 11 at the age of thirty-five. She followed the captain's first wife into the rocky Texas soil.

The location of her grave is unknown. When Fort Stockton closed for the final time, the burials from the post cemetery were relocated to the Sam Houston National Cemetery. Laura is not named among these, although the list includes the note, "Unknown, a woman in a fine casket."

Captain Carpenter soon left Fort Stockton as federal troops departed the state following the secession of Texas. With the war's outbreak, he joined Union forces in the western theater, becoming a major in the Nineteenth Infantry. He died leading a heroic effort against the Confederate assault at Stones River, Tennessee. His body made its way back to Maine to be buried beside his infant son, who died a few months after his birth.

A few days after his wife's death, Captain Carpenter sat down in the rude home he and Laura had shared and began a letter to relatives informing them of her death. He wrote, "Our bright and beautiful Laura is no more."

Kiotas, Musk Hogs and Umbras

With the secession of Texas in 1861 and the withdrawal of federal troops, the challenge of frontier defense fell on the Confederacy, in reality on Texas. John S. Ford was commissioned to organize a regiment of state troopers who became the Second Texas Cavalry. Various volunteer units were recruited for this duty.

At the war's outbreak, many Texas communities formed volunteer units. One these was the W.P. Lane Rangers (named in honor of a local hero), organized in Marshall, Texas. The Rangers were recruited to reenlist in the Confederate army and reluctantly agreed to serve on the frontier for one year. They were mustered into Confederate service as Company F, Second Regiment Texas Mounted Rifles, on May 23, 1861. Over the next year, small detachments of the rangers were assigned to the western Texas forts—Camp Hudson, Fort Clark, Fort Inge and Fort Lancaster.

One of the Fort Lancaster soldiers created an unusual, detailed and entertaining account of his Confederate service. William Williston Heartsill maintained a journal throughout the war using small notebooks, each of which was sent home when filled. Following the war's end, he collected them into a book. Heartsill printed one hundred copies on a hand-operated press. *Fourteen Hundred and 91 Days in the Confederate Army* (the length of his service) is fascinating reading, providing invaluable insight into the thoughts and deeds of a common Civil War soldier.

The first detail of Company F arrived at Fort Lancaster on November 6. Heartsill followed with a second group, arriving on December 3, bringing the command to seventy-five, led by two lieutenants. They were almost all young men under the age of twenty-five, many of whom had never been this far from home.

Duty at the fort was light. Eight men were assigned daily to oversee the grazing horse herd and guard them in the corral at night. Like all young men with plenty of free time, they developed their own amusements to pass the time. They played "Town-Ball" (a precursor of modern baseball) and spent evenings shooting and trapping the numerous "kiotas" that gathered around the post every evening. They enjoyed an evening concert by fellow soldier Louis Attaway, who played a fife, accompanied by eight "umbras" (Mexican "hombres") singing Spanish songs and dancing.

They never faced any serious threats. The only Indian they saw was a young Apache child captured in New Mexico traveling with troops passing through from El Paso. The greatest hazards during their Lancaster service were the chilling winds and sleet of bitterly cold "northers" and a live musk hog brought into camp, "a grizzly, savage, one hundred and twenty pound institution" that could be viewed for one chew of "flat" tobacco. Their only casualty was the death of Joseph Norris from pneumonia.

Their most creative diversion occurred when General H.H. Sibley passed through on his way to New Mexico. Sibley had been commissioned to lead an expedition to secure Arizona and New Mexico for the Confederacy, an effort that failed with the defeat of Sibley's brigade at Glorietta Pass in New Mexico the following year.

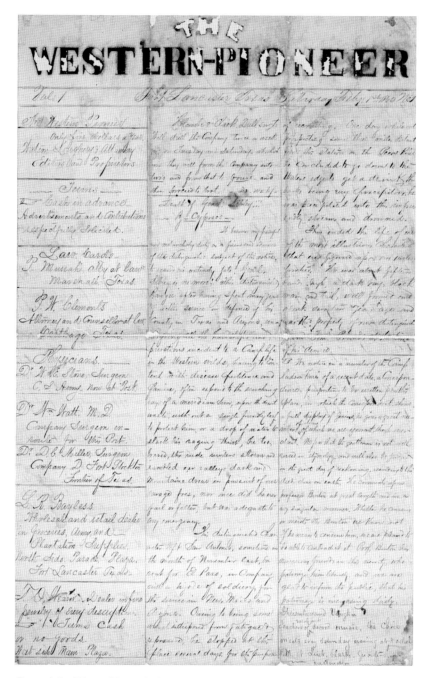

Copy of the *Western Pioneer. Author's collection.*

Sibley passed through Fort Lancaster on November 28. The fort detail turned out in uniform, mounted for review by the general. As the troops passed in front of Sibley, he gave the order "file left," which was "of course" unheard. The Lancaster detail continued at a brisk trot and ascended the nearby mountain. As they disappeared out of sight, the general muttered, "Gone to Hell." When the company returned that evening, they found that Sibley had "gone on his way rejoicing to New Mexico."

They also filled their leisure time by publishing a newspaper. During their frontier time, the rangers produced two newspapers, the *Camp Hudson Times* and the *Western Pioneer* at Fort Lancaster. The "editors" created each handwritten edition, from which copies were made. Some copies were sent home, and one or two survived. Heartsill also printed an example of each in his book.

Heartsill admitted that the papers were "on the burlesque order" but were eagerly awaited by the local readers. Watson, Attaway and Company edited the *Western Pioneer*, for "only five dollars a year, no cash desired or expected." The paper included the latest news from El Paso, editorials regarding the Confederate cause, a piece describing western Texas and original poetry of questionable quality. Advertisements from the local "businesses" were solicited and printed—"Hudson & Co. Dealers in Musk Hogs." Harwell and Company operated the "Menger Hotel" near the commissary with a fare of "beef brains and chicken feet, musk hog and coffee cakes, freeholder beans, and weevil eaten crackers."

Heartsill left Fort Lancaster in early February 1862 as part of a fifteen-man detail to Camp Hudson. The remaining rangers followed at the beginning of April. Their time on the frontier ended, the W.P. Lane Rangers rode eastward for more active service and three years of bloody battles, prison camps and defeat. Behind them, the Texas frontier was abandoned to the Native Americans who chose to venture there.

THE LAWFUL AND THE LAWLESS

The Pecos River Country is a harsh, unforgiving landscape that can quickly prove deadly to those failing to respect its dangers. To live here for any amount of time, one must develop a flinty measure of toughness that burns away pretense. Many residents develop a steadfast, trustworthy character that makes them "someone to ride the river with." Others, however, turn as mean and bitter as the river's alkaline waters. The Pecos River Country molds them all—the lawful, the lawless and those somewhere in between.

THE FEUD

When Reeves County sheriff Bud Frazer hired Jim Miller as a deputy, he had no idea that he was employing his future killer. The origins of a bloody feud that spread across two counties began with that decision.

Bud Frazer was elected sheriff of Reeves County in 1890. That same year, a handsome, well-dressed young man arrived in Pecos City. Polite, well-mannered Jim Miller was soon well liked by many in the community. He joined the Methodist church; seldom smoke, drank or cussed; and earned the nickname "Deacon." Based on several recommendations, Frazer made Miller a deputy. What few knew then was that Miller was already a notorious hired killer who most likely even murdered his own

Bud Frazier stands on the far left in this 1883 photograph taken in Pecos City. *Fort Stockton Historical Society Archives.*

grandparents. On man who knew Miller well said of him, "He was just a killer—the worst man I ever knew."

The relationship did not last long. Miller soon became suspected of cattle rustling in the area. Among the accusing cattlemen was Barney Riggs of Fort Stockton, brother-in-law to Sheriff Frazer. Riggs was himself a similar gunman—polite and well-mannered but deadly when provoked. Serving time for murder in the infamous Yuma, Arizona prison, Riggs earned a pardon if he promised to leave the territory. He joined his family in Pecos County in 1888. A few years later, he married Annie Frazer Johnson, Sheriff Frazer's sister.

Riggs stated his belief that Miller was responsible for the cattle thefts, which Miller denied, and enmity began between the two. As evidence mounted, Frazer eventually fired Miller, who then managed to become Pecos City marshal. Miller began plotting Frazer's assassination, recruiting two gunmen to assist him. The plot was uncovered, but the conspirators were acquitted.

Frazer decided to deal with Miller himself. In April 1894, he confronted Miller on a Pecos City street. In the ensuing gunbattle, Frazer shot Miller in the chest, the bullet bouncing off the steel breastplate Miller wore under his clothes. A second shot struck his right arm. Miller attempted to fire with his left but missed. Frazer's third shot hit Miller's leg. Frazer left Miller alive, unaware that the breastplate had saved him.

The violence cost Frazer his job. Bitter, he moved to New Mexico. Miller bragged that he had run Frazer off and continued plotting to kill him. In December 1894, Frazer returned to Pecos City to visit his sister and Barney. He confronted Miller in a second gunfight, hitting him several times in the chest, with Miller's metal breastplate again saving him. Frazer was arrested and tried in El Paso but acquitted.

Having lost two gunfights, Miller now planned Bud Frazer's murder. On September 14, 1896, while Frazer was playing cards in a saloon in Toyah, Miller made his move. Stepping into the saloon with a double-barrel shotgun, he shot Frazer in the face, blowing away most of his head. After firing the second barrel as well, Miller calmly reloaded his shotgun and claimed that Frazer had drawn on him. Miller's crony in the saloon backed up his assertion.

The Johnson and Heard Saloon in Pecos City. *Fort Stockton Historical Society Archives.*

Miller now sought to kill Barney Riggs. He recruited William Earhart and John Denson for the job. Hearing of the plot, Riggs was unintimidated. Told of the bulletproof vests worn by Miller and possibly other gang members, Barney replied that he would shoot both in the head. He drove his family to safety with relatives, Annie riding with a shotgun in her lap.

Riggs confronted Earhart and Denson in the Johnson and Heard Saloon in Pecos City on October 3, 1896, waiting for them to make the first move. As all three stood at the bar, Earhart drew his pistol. Riggs was faster, shooting him in the face. Earhart was dead before he struck the floor. Denson made a grab for Earhart's pistol on the floor but panicked and backed toward the saloon door. Riggs shot him through the head before he reached it. Staggering outside, Denson died seconds later. Barney calmly returned to the bar and called for a drink. Miller fled the area. Riggs was tried for the shooting and acquitted. The feud was over.

Barney Riggs met his own violent end. Tired of her difficult, abusive and dangerous marriage to Riggs, Annie divorced him in 1901. Buck Chadborn, her son-in-law, helped administer the contentious settlement. Barney was uncooperative, intimidating Chadborn. On April 8, mistakenly thinking that Barney was reaching for a gun, Buck shot him. Barney Riggs was carried to the Koehler Hotel in Fort Stockton, where he died an hour later, cursing Chadborn to the last.

THE TRUE LAW WEST OF THE PECOS

Judge Roy Bean may have posted the sign above his saloon and handed down interesting rulings, but another Pecos County official also laid claim to the title "law west of the Pecos." His name was Dud Barker.

When thirty-one-year-old Dudley S. Barker rode into Fort Stockton to take the job of sheriff in 1904, Pecos County was still a frontier land. Some two hundred miles in extent, it reached south to the Rio Grande River. Roads were still primitive; the Southern Pacific Railroad crossed the county sixty long miles from the county seat. Ten years earlier, a former Pecos County sheriff had been killed in the courthouse, and the case remained unsolved.

A group of Fort Stockton leaders had ridden to Barker's ranch near Sanderson to ask him to run for Pecos County sheriff. They knew of his reputation as a Texas Ranger and believed that he was the man they wanted to bring law and order to the sprawling county.

Barker joined Frontier Battalion Company B under the command of the famous W.J. McDonald in 1896 at the age of twenty-three. He served two years in the Rangers. During that time, he was among those sent to San Saba to deal with the lawlessness and murder caused by the San Saba Mob, who had ruled the town for years. Despite mob efforts, the Rangers accumulated enough evidence to bring them before a grand jury. When mob members attempted to prevent the Rangers from entering the court, a shootout resulted in which one masked mobster was killed and the rest dispersed. In the ensuing trial, several mobsters were convicted and sent to prison, breaking their stranglehold on San Saba.

Barker served as Pecos County sheriff for twenty-three years. Almost six feet tall, the fearless and efficient lawman always carried a single pistol during his time in office. He was never afraid to use it. As one old cowboy recalled, Dud brought law and order with him, and he kept it. He began his first term by shutting down an illegal poker game of several prominent townspeople. He told the players to pay their fines without any challenge. They did.

Impressed by a young Pecos River cowboy who singlehandedly tracked and captured several horse thieves on his own initiative, Barker recruited

Sheriff Dud Barker in his Pecos County office in 1905. *Fort Stockton Historical Society Archives.*

him for the Texas Rangers. On April 21, 1905, twenty-two-year-old Frank Hamer was sworn in as a Texas Ranger at Sheffield.

Barker kept a Winchester rifle on his saddle. When he bought one of Fort Stockton's first automobiles, he mounted a rifle and shotgun in it. The number of men he is reputed to have killed varies. One of his deputies placed the number at twenty-two. Though unafraid of a fight, Barker was a cautious man. He walked down the center of the street, constantly watching, and sat with his back to the wall. That may help explain why he was never wounded in any of his numerous gun battles.

One particularly deadly fight took place on the evening of November 8, 1912. A group of drunken Mexican railroad workers took a deputy's gun and shot at him. Barker confronted the workers in the cantina and, in the gunfight that erupted, killed at least four, although some placed the number higher. No one questioned if the men were armed or had drawn on the sheriff.

Gunfights were not the only instances where Barker enforced the law by his own standard of justice. More than one rowdy found himself in jail for the offense of "raising hell." On one arrest, Barker simply noted that the prisoner was "a bad man." Despite the feeling among some in the Mexican community that Barker dealt out justice unfairly, his wife, Lilly, remained a popular and respected member of the local Catholic church.

Barker and his family lived in the bottom floor of the county jail; the prisoners were locked upstairs. He treated his prisoners well and would enlist them in working on the jail grounds to pay off fines. He took pride in the beautiful hedges, grass, flowers and trees surrounding the jail.

With the coming of Prohibition, Barker aggressively pursued bootleggers, even if they proved to be prominent citizens. His policy was, "I don't make the laws; I just enforce them." He boasted that Pecos County was the driest in the United States and had a standing offer of $100 for anyone who could buy a quart of liquor in his county.

Barker's sometimes unorthodox style, his Prohibition work and complaints about questionable actions by his deputies eventually led to his defeat. As one writer phrased it, "With his fast friends, he also had fast enemies." Barker was defeated by Will Rooney, member of a local pioneer family, by a narrow margin in 1926.

On December 31, 1926, Barker loaded all the family's belongings from the jail. Just before midnight, with help, he cut every tree, hedge and flower to the ground and left them lying there. Then former sheriff Barker departed for his new home in Alpine.

End of the Tall Texan

As the westbound Galveston, Harrisburg and San Antonio no. 91 train left the brief Dryden stop on the night of March 12, 1912, a tall man slipped out of the shadows and jumped aboard the engine. Cap pulled low and a dark handkerchief over his face, he pointed an automatic pistol at the train crew, warning them, "Do as I tell you and you won't be hurt."

Halfway between Dryden and Sanderson, the tracks crossed a long bridge over a deep canyon. The bandit ordered the train stopped. Four whistle blasts sounded. A second masked bandit climbed aboard and covered the engine crew. The tall man forced other train crew to uncouple the engine, baggage and express cars and move them down the track, stranding any passengers aboard. These included sixty troopers of the U.S. Army Third Cavalry and Deputy Sheriff Dan Farley of Sanderson, who only then realized that something was wrong. So far, the robbery was going smoothly. That would soon change.

The tall bandit was the infamous outlaw Ben Kilpatrick, nicknamed the "Tall Texan" for his six-foot, two-inch height. The native Texan chose a criminal career over cowboying. Kilpatrick rode with the Ketchum Gang, robbing trains in New Mexico. Fleeing a failed robbery, he joined the Wild Bunch Gang in Utah and Wyoming. Also including Butch Cassidy, the Sundance Kid and Will Carver, the Wild Bunch became the most successful train robbers in the West.

In 1901, the gang robbed the Great Northern Train in Montana, making off with $70,000. Returning to Texas, Kilpatrick survived a shootout in Sonora, Texas, where Will Carver was killed. The Tall Texan and lover Laura Bullion were arrested later that year in St. Louis with part of the Great Northern robbery money. Kilpatrick was found guilty of robbery and sentenced to fifteen years in prison.

Released in 1911, in part because of a petition to President Taft to pardon him that circulated across several West Texas counties and garnered several thousand signatures, Kilpatrick came to Sheffield, where two of his brothers lived. Boone Kilpatrick owned a ranch south of town, and his brother Felix worked on different ranches. Sheffield was also home to Berry Ketchum. While Ketchum was known as an honest man, his two brothers, Sam and Tom "Black Jack," were outlaws, eventually perishing at the hands of the law.

The small community had a reputation as a tough place. Its location near the border of three Texas counties, miles from the all three county seats, meant that law officers were frequently far away. Young Walter Fulcher, who worked on a ranch near the Kilpatricks, often saw Ben over the next few months, along with Ole Hobek, the second train bandit. Though just out of prison, the tall man wore an expensive Stetson hat and clothes, the money probably coming from several recent local small bank robberies. Fulcher remembered, "He was handsome in a dark, sinister way, and I think he could have made more money in the movies than by robbing trains."

With the train successfully isolated, Kilpatrick forced Wells Fargo agent David Trousdale to open the mail car and began searching packages. He found little. One held two dollars and another thirty-five. While he searched, he took delight in jabbing Trousdale with his pistol, repeatedly telling him to raise his arms higher. Angered, the unarmed Truesdale complied, looking for a chance to change things.

While Kilpatrick opened packages in the express car, Trousdale spotted a wooden maul atop a barrel of oysters. The heavy mallet-like tool used for breaking up ice was a formidable weapon. Trousdale secreted the maul under his coat. He kept "jollying" the robber along to gain his confidence.

When Trousdale pointed to some packages Kilpatrick had overlooked, the bandit stooped to examine them. Trousdale struck him a hard blow to the back of his skull, breaking his neck. Kilpatrick went down with a slight groan. Trousdale hit him two more times. On the third blow, the maul crashed through his skull, spattering the outlaw's brains over the side of the car.

Trousdale quickly removed two Colt pistols from the body and armed the mail clerks. He took the Winchester rifle and turned out the gas lights in the car. He fired a round through the top of the car to attract the other bandit.

The shot drew Hobek, who came down the train calling, "Frank! Frank! What's the matter?" When he opened the express car door, Trousdale shot him in the head, killing him instantly. What he did not know at the time was that Hobek had six sticks of dynamite and a bottle of nitroglycerine on him. Had his shot hit any of those, they would have all been blown to pieces. An additional one hundred pounds of explosives were found nearby.

The passenger cars were reconnected, and the train continued to Sanderson, arriving in the early morning. The dead bodies of Ben Kilpatrick and Ole Hobek were propped up by the train crew for a photograph.

Trousdale was hailed as a hero. He received a $1,000 reward, a $250 gold watch and a promotion for his actions. Several vaudeville companies made him offers as high as $100 per week, but he refused them all.

Train crew posing with the bodies of Ben Kilpatrick (*left*) and Ole Hobek. *Wikimedia Commons.*

Kilpatrick and Hobek were wrapped in sheets and buried in Sanderson in a single box. The attempted robbery at Baxter's Curve was among the last train robberies in Texas and the final one for the Tall Texan.

El Presidente

Joe Madero was an unusual kind of outlaw—unless he wasn't an outlaw at all.

The individual most people knew as Joe Madero arrived in Sheffield around 1915 or a bit earlier; no one remembers exactly. In his mid-forties, he was, at first, reluctant to reveal much about himself. Some thought that he was hiding out. He spoke only a few words of English. He found part-time work on area ranches, sheepherding or managing stock, frequently on Sam Murray's place.

Joe eventually became an excellent wool packer, or wool tramper. As the sheep-shearing crews trimmed the wool, it was tossed into large burlap bags hung in a wooden frame constructed to hold them. Before the bag was sealed, the wool needed to be packed down as compactly as possible. Joe was small, around five-foot-seven, and slender in build. He easily fit down into the bag, dancing around, tightly packing the wool.

Joe lived alone in a small adobe house on the east end of Sheffield. No family or acquaintances ever came to visit. He seemed to have no past. As he grew older, that changed. Joe eventually revealed bits of his history. He claimed he had been president of Mexico during the revolution that began in 1910, or perhaps he was almost president. The stories varied over the years.

Joe claimed that he came to Sheffield from Mexico. He was a brother to Francisco Madero, the short-lived president of the Mexican republic during the revolutionary years. Madero's enemies eventually took him prisoner and executed him. Joe claimed that he was also captured and brutally tortured, the scars of which he still bore. He escaped, however, and made his way to the border and to this remote West Texas town, where he felt safe enough to remain. If he ever returned, he would certainly be killed. His claims eventually earned him the nickname "El Presidente."

As Joe's story became more widely known in the small town, even the children became familiar with it. Perhaps a few even believed it. Most considered them tall tales. Everyone humored Joe in his delusions, more for the man they knew than the one he professed to be.

Joe had highly gracious, formal manners. When he met folks on the street, he often bowed politely, perhaps greeting with a small bit of English, a "good morning" or "good evening." He had a friendly word for all, a smile beneath the little reddish-colored mustache he wore for years. He earned a second nickname, "Joe Politeness."

When younger, he played the guitar and French harp and often sang for different groups. He loved to dance, offering to dance an hour for a dime. One Christmas season, he performed a memorable Mexican hat dance at the old Texaco station, a favorite local gathering spot. Tossing his hat on the ground, he executed an elaborate dance, deftly twisting and turning.

When Joe lost his stamina for wool packing, he turned to another source of income: his landholdings. As a member of the Madero family, Joe claimed that he was heir to the Sheffield land. He made his rounds each month, visiting homes and businesses, requesting his "rent." He carried a large ring of keys he claimed were the keys to everything in town. People gave him dimes or quarters in the Depression years, later raising the amount to a dollar or two.

Joe never asked for food or other goods, only the rent to which he was entitled. He carried a little receipt book with him on his rounds and gladly wrote out receipts for all who requested one, inscribed in eloquent Spanish, filled with curves and flourishes. He made enough for his basic needs. The rest he gave away.

Many afternoons, Joe sat waiting on the wide cement porch of Sandel's Mercantile Store. When the little school bus arrived from nearby Iraan in a cloud of West Texas dust, the children, upon seeing him, began shouting "El Presidente!" Joe would stand, grandly sweep off his hat and then bow deeply, the tip of his hat lightly brushing the dusty street. As they descended the bus and surrounded him, it did not matter whether they spoke in mockery or respect. He dug into his pockets for nickels and dimes, generously handing them out to be exchanged for sodas and ice cream in the store, a welcome treat for these Depression-era children.

Joe died in Sheffield on July 31, 1958, at the age of eighty-nine and was laid to rest at the local cemetery. The name on his death certificate was Valentine Rubio. Few knew him by that name.

So, was there any truth to Joe's claim? There are a few interesting traces. Francisco Madero did have several brothers, though none named Jose. His brother Gustavo was tortured but then brutally killed. Madero was assassinated in 1913, and Joe arrived in Sheffield around 1915.

Joe Madero on the porch of the old Sheffield mercantile store. *Author's collection.*

Francisco and Joe (or Valentine) were both small and lean in stature. Both loved to dance. Both had great hearts for children. Both evidenced manners and language that implied an upper-class background.

Perhaps more intriguingly, Madero was a spiritualist, believing in communication with the dead. He claimed to communicate with the spirit of a brother who died as a child. In 1907, a second spirit, identifying himself as Jose (interesting!), began to give him guidance that led him to launch his bid for power.

Small communities often have a local eccentric professing to be someone more famous. The Granbury saloonkeeper who claimed to be John Wilkes Booth. Brushy Bill Roberts of Hico, who swore that he was Billy the Kid. The skeptic in us smiles knowingly at such fanciful assertions. Yet there often remains that bit of wondering, "But what if…?" I like to think that, if we had asked old Joe who he really was, he would have smiled, shrugged his shoulders and replied, "Quien sabe? Quizas." Who knows? Perhaps.

FIRST LADY

Loving County, a relatively small slice of Texas lying just south of New Mexico and east of the Pecos River, has some interesting distinctions. Not only is it the least populated county in Texas, reporting only sixty-four residents in the 2020 census, but it is also the least populous county in the entire United States. Created in 1887 from Tom Green County, it was the only Texas county to have been organized twice. After several years under the jurisdiction of Reeves County, an election in 1893 created a separate county organization, apparently part of a fraudulent irrigation scheme by a Denver, Colorado group. With no recognizable county government and legal county residents, the county was de-organized and reattached to Reeves County. When oil production in the 1920s brought people into the county, it was organized a second time in 1931. The population grew to a booming six hundred by 1933, eventually declining to its current numbers. The county's more reputable claim to fame is that it elected the first woman sheriff in the state of Texas in 1945.

Edna Reed Clayton Dewees came to Mentone in 1944 to serve as a deputy in the Loving County tax office for Sheriff Hardin Ross. The twenty-three-year-old brought a considerable body of experience with her. She had served as deputy district clerk in Stephens County, Texas. She had also operated a lathe in a Fort Worth aircraft manufacturing plant. Before coming to Mentone, she served at the Special Services Office at the Pecos Army Airfield in Pecos, Texas.

She had been in her new position only a short time when things changed dramatically. Sheriff Ross resigned his position and recommended that Dewees be appointed sheriff and tax assessor-collector. In January 1945, the commissioners court approved his request, and Dewees became the sheriff of Loving County. This made her the second woman in Texas to serve as sheriff.

Emma Bannister was the wife of John Bannister, who was elected Coleman County sheriff in 1914. She, John and their nine children lived on the first floor of the county jail. Besides managing the large family, Emma served as John's office deputy. When John died of a stroke in August 1918, the county election was only a few months away. The county commissioners felt that everything would work out best if Emma could finish her husband's term. She became Texas's first woman sheriff.

When election time arrived in Loving County in 1945, Dewees ran for the office and easily won. At age twenty-four, she became the first elected female sheriff in Texas. She served until 1947. After serving as Loving County sheriff, Dewees became county district clerk in Loving from 1965 to 1986.

Sheriff Dewees stayed active during her term. The county was bustling, with several major oil companies working in the area that often housed workers in camps. Times were not dangerous, however. Sheriff Dewees never wore a gun. "I knew everyone," she said. She made only two arrests in a county known for its low crime rate. Recordkeeping proved the greatest headache in a time of cumbersome calculators and carbon paper records. The courthouse had the only phone in the county but lacked air conditioning.

As sheriff and a longtime Mentone resident, Dewees was known for her generous nature. Her focus was always the school and community. She worked to put eyeglasses on every needy child in the district. She made certain that anyone from Loving County had the proper clothing and shoes for any special occasion they attended. Edna Dewees was not only the first elected woman sheriff; she was also a classy lady.

THE HUNTED AND
THE HUNTERS

B eing an active treasure hunter requires three important things: time
to hunt, access to the territory where you want to hunt and, most
importantly, an unshakeable belief that what you hunt *may* actually be out
there. Despite any amount of evidence to the contrary—illogical tales, the
weight of gold and silver bars, secondhand deathbed accounts—facts are
simply things arrayed in support of your quest or evidence to be discarded
if they hinder your hunt. Historian and folklorist Paul Patterson phrased it
best: "The fact that history may be a bit hazy lends more credence to the
legend....Besides, treasure hunters are hunting treasure, not history."

A big, remote, rugged and mostly empty place like the Pecos Country
attracts tales of lost riches like a magnet does iron filings. No matter
how illogical or tenuous the accounts, they survive repeated tellings and
revisions. And again, like magnets, the stories attract certain dreamers who
develop a particular fascination, many would consider obsession, for them.
They spend countless hours poring over old accounts or wandering the
landscape, always in search of that marking, that alignment, that small
cave that leads them to the treasure. To the rest of us, they appear a bit
insane. To other true believers, they are people of vision.

Legendary Castle Gap, the focus of many Pecos Country treasure tales. *Photograph by author.*

THERE IS A MAP

A group of former soldiers are hired on as guards with a wagon train and discover they are escorting a treasure. A wandering Spanish expedition decides to bury some of the gold they carry. A party of priests flees into the Pecos Country with fifteen burros loaded with stolen treasures. An old man chased by the Rangers hides in a cave in a Y-shaped valley and finds a pile of silver bars, the ruins of a stage or wagon not far away.

The guards murder the wagon party, burn the bodies and wagons and hide the treasure. The priests bury their treasure on a mountain, disguising it as a Native American grave, and swear never to disturb it. The old man memorizes the terrain and takes two silver bars, perhaps weighing a total of 140 pounds.

The priests travel many miles before they carve cryptic directions into a large rock to help them relocate the treasure, along with false ones to confuse other seekers. The Spaniards also inscribe clues to their treasure's location—somewhere. The outlaw band is slaughtered by Indians, except for a sole survivor. On his deathbed, he recounts his treasure story and draws a crude map. The old man is captured and jailed in San Antonio. What happened to the silver he carried is not recorded. Sick and dying, he draws a crude map from memory and gives it to the jailer who treated him kindly.

Tales of lost treasures often follow a similar narrative. Treasure found or stolen—treasure hidden. Clues left—maps drawn and passed on. When the treasure hunters go in search of the lost wealth, something goes wrong. The landscape appears different. Things have changed. The clues are unclear. Sometimes, someone may have discovered the treasure first.

While cryptic carvings, natural or man-made, can often be discovered on the mesas along the Pecos, the fragile treasure maps usually do not survive. Instead, they become part of the lost legends themselves. In one case, that did not happen.

The map made by the old man who found a cave of silver bars has supposedly endured through time. The San Antonio jailer kept it for more than twenty years but never made it west. He finally passed it along to a friend who lived near the small Pecos River town of Sheffield. Three generations of that family have handed it down.

In the early 1960s, Ed Syers wrote of the map in a collection of his columns titled *Off the Beaten Trail*. Syers visited with local Pecos County constable Allen Graham, who then owned the map. Graham agreed to show Syers the map.

Carefully unfolding the fragile piece of thin paper aged by time, Graham pointed out the features on the map indicating an old route from the Pecos to Fort Concho and San Angelo. A line marks the road from Fort Stockton, crossing the Pecos at Pontoon Crossing and continuing to Santa Rita. The Santa Rita well struck oil in 1923, launching the Permian Basin oil industry. The well's location was not far from Grierson's Springs, a stop on the trail from Forts Concho to Stockton. It makes a curious mixture of frontier history and more modern times. Was Santa Rita there when the old man found the treasure or simply used as a later reference point? For that matter, when did his discovery take place?

Below the road, there are some wavy lines and a series of crescent moon–shaped figures, with the notation "cave" at one end. These are said to indicate a Y-shaped valley, located a few miles north of Iraan. Another spot marks "old irons."

Graham told Syers that his grandfather found those old wagon irons, some rusted guns and a packsaddle. As for the cave? The rimrocks of the mesa are filled with any number of shallow holes eroded from the limestone. Y-shaped valleys are a common feature of the region. Which is the correct one? Which "cave" is filled with silver?

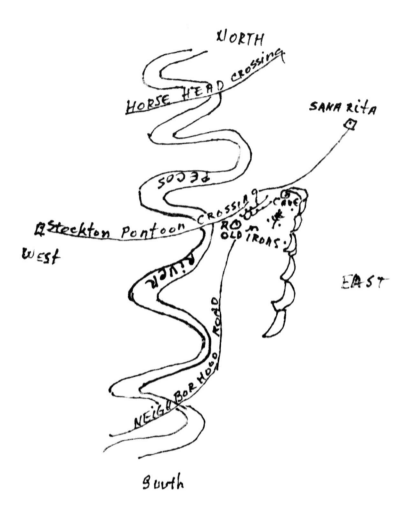

Facsimile copy of an old treasure map. *From Pecos County History.*

Jim Jones of nearby McCamey was among those who spent years searching for the cave until landowners became tired of the treasure hunters disrupting the ranch work. Today, most ranches keep their gates locked. No one ever claimed to have found the treasure.

So, there is one treasure map. It still exists, handed down another generation from Constable Graham. You will probably never get a look at it. However, you can find a copy of it in the Pecos County history, published in 1984, if you want to try your luck. If it is even an accurate copy.

You will need three things....

THE IRON HORSE

I knew one of those West Texas treasure seekers. I even went in search of treasure with him.

Lester Baxter worked as a mechanic at the Hale Garage in Sheffield in the 1950s and '60s. Pretty much everyone knew him by his last name. A bachelor, his companions were a few old dogs. His major vice was alcohol, which consumed his money and health. His passion, however, was hunting treasure.

Baxter had no doubt that there was some sort of treasure somewhere out there in the Pecos River Country. Too many folks—from Spaniards to soldiers and outlaws—had passed through, carrying all sorts of potential riches, for there to be nothing. There were simply too many tales, too many interesting marks in the landscape. Something lay hidden out there, along with clues to its location. You just had to keep searching until you found it.

As a young teenager in the 1960s, I always knew him as Baxter. Sheffield was a small stop on the Old Spanish Trail Highway (U.S. 290), which ran coast to coast, boasting perhaps three hundred souls. Baxter was one of the regulars at the local restaurant where my parents worked. He enjoyed sharing his latest thoughts on treasure with any who were interested, although he, of course, always keep key details to himself.

I always had a love of history and must have shown a special interest in his tales because he eventually invited me along on one of his expeditions. I was also probably cheap labor to help with the digging.

One memorable day, we loaded his metal detector and some tools into his old pickup (black, as I recall) and set out. We crossed the Pecos into Crockett County on Highway 290 and, a few miles farther east, turned north on the county road along Live Oak Creek. We crossed the creek on the concrete slab that marked part of the original OST route. Not far from there, we went through an old wire gate and turned back south along the creek on a rough pasture road running between the creek and the base of the mountain. A few rugged miles brought us to a relatively level spot. I did not see much there, but Baxter pointed out a few rocks that might have once marked the foundation of some structure. How Baxter had ever discovered this place I do not recall. Someone had been here, but who or when was quite unclear.

One small piece of limestone, embedded on edge, did have some lines incised on it. We got down beside it and tried to match them to the horizon line, but we did not have much luck.

We broke out the metal detector and began to scan the area. Almost immediately, we had high-pitched beeps directing us. After uncovering

Toy horse found on a treasure hunt. *Photograph by author.*

several bits of metal and old nails, we hit on a spot that gave a larger reading. Something big must be down there!

Excited, we began digging, following the signal into the earth. The hole grew larger and wider as we went down. I recall it reaching several feet square. The signal continued, the caliche soil getting tougher to dig, but we struck nothing large. Eventually, we concluded that something in the soil itself was giving the reading. When pointed at the excavated dirt, the detector responded. We had a false reading, perhaps caused by oxides or minerals in the soil. Baxter concluded that perhaps we were digging where horses or other animals had been kept and their urine had saturated the soil enough to mislead us.

Disappointed, we filled our treasure hole and left with no riches. However, to me, we did find a treasure. A bit below the surface, we uncovered a small metal toy. It was a horse, made of two narrow pieces of metal pressed together. Some six inches long, it runs in full stride, although parts of two legs are gone. The tail is also gone, but I imagine it once streamed proudly behind. There is the trace of an eye, short ears, perhaps a nostril. I kept that toy horse; Baxter had no interest in it. I still have it all these years later. I still wonder about the tale it could tell.

A toy implies family, a child, a horse perhaps—more than a boy's toy. Where we dug had once been home to someone long enough for this small toy to end up in the ground. Was it a special toy, perhaps an only one? Was it lost or cast away? Were they immigrants on the old stage and wagon road? Was it a pioneer ranching family? A small iron horse is all that remains of their life in this place. The rest is a mystery.

Baxter never found the treasures he sought. His drinking eventually led him to a lonely and tragic end. I will always appreciate him taking me in search of treasure. On that trip, I found one. I am sorry he never did.

84

WILD RIVER

Before years of irrigation and dams, the Pecos of prior centuries was a far more lethal version than the present river. No one will ever know exactly how many lives it claimed over the years, victims of raging floods, crumbling riverbanks, steep cliffs and alkaline waters. Native Americans, cowboys, unlucky travelers, swimmers and illegal migrants have all perished in the river.

Even as modern crossings improved journeys and various dams and irrigation projects grew along the river, it could still create havoc at times. Two floods in 1893 caused major damage and changed the course of the river. They would not be the last. The Pecos today runs more slowly and presents little barrier to modern travelers. Yet when abnormal rains fall, the river still rampages, adding new chapters to its deadly reputation.

The Vanishing Falls

If you stop in the small town of Grandfalls and ask any longtime resident the location of the falls, they will tell you that there are no falls. Once, they were real enough to inspire the community's name. They have been gone for quite a long time, however. No one living has ever seen them. The story of their passing is woven within the tale of the founding of Grandfalls.

When major irrigation projects began along the Texas Pecos River in 1888, there were two sets of falls on the river. The Grand Falls were located about three miles south of the future community of Grandfalls. Eight miles upstream from them were the Great Falls, located near where the counties of Pecos and Reeves meet at the Pecos River.

In 1889, the Texas legislature passed a bill to encourage irrigation and for the right to "use of water for canals, ditches, flumes, reservoirs, and wells for irrigation." Even before the passage of SHB No. 298, the Pioneer Canal Company began construction of a canal. Others soon launched additional agricultural ventures.

Several members of the Hardeman family began development of the Pecos near the falls, helping pioneer the Grandfalls Irrigation Company in 1890. The company built a low brush dam along the Great Falls to divert water into an irrigation canal. In those early years, the valley and community that arose were sometimes referred to as "Great Falls."

The canal carried water down the valley to irrigate crops of cotton, corn and alfalfa. Lee Hardeman built the first gin on this stretch of the river. It was operated by waterpower, with mule power running the press. The cotton was carried from the wagons to the one-stand gin in willow baskets. Hardeman also operated a gristmill to grind corn.

Settlers began moving into the valley, farmers and land investors acquiring land along the river valley. The fledgling community of Grandfalls began to grow. The irrigation company built the first school, and a "union" church served the faithful.

The Pecos, largely untamed at that time, was subject to destructive floods. The year 1893 proved especially deadly. In early August, the river waters rose ten feet above normal in New Mexico. The flood swept downstream, destroying dams and covering the Texas and Pacific railroad bridge to a depth of seven feet, stopping all trains for ten days. Numerous chickens and livestock drowned. Farmer J.J. Miller of Barstow lost five hundred acres of alfalfa when they sat underwater for five days. In the Grandfalls area, several families fled their homes moments ahead of the rising waters. Colonel R.C. Carr was preparing for dinner when a frantic rider arrived to warn him to get out quickly. "I looked out and saw the water coming in a wall seven feet high and just rolling, and my hunger left me."

At the Great Falls dam, Lee Hardeman feared that the water would wash away the brush dam. To relieve the pressure on the dam, he plowed several furrows across the bend of the Pecos above the falls to a point below them to create a path for some of the excess water. Once this was accomplished,

Site of the Great Falls, June 1961. *Ward County Archives.*

the unexpected happened. The Pecos changed course along the new path, leaving the Great Falls high and dry.

The loss of the Great Falls was devastating to the local farmers. A number chose to leave. To survive, the Grandfalls Irrigation Company, using mule power, constructed a new dam two miles upstream from the falls and extended the canal an extra two miles. The Hardemans had had enough, however, and sold their interests in the irrigation company, the gin and the gristmill.

In February 1894, Horace Smith acquired land near the Grand Falls and built the valley's second water-powered gin beside them. To gain even more power for his gin, Smith built a race around the falls. For several years, he was quite successful, until the Pecos struck again. A 1900 flood hit the head works of the race, which gave way. The river poured down the race, again altering its path. The Grand Falls, like the Great Falls, were gone.

THE 1954 FLOOD

When rains come hard and fast, the shallow soil and steep rocky canyons of the lower Pecos drain rapidly, pouring torrents of water into the river. In a matter of minutes, the river becomes a raging torrent, sowing destruction in its path. The summer of 1954 was especially damaging, producing the most expensive bridge disaster in Texas history.

On Thursday, June 24, a tropical storm rapidly developed in the western Gulf of Mexico. By the following day, it was Hurricane Alice. Moving inland in northern Mexico, the storm tracked northwest along the Texas-Mexico border for several days. Twenty-eight inches of rain fell into the Pecos drainage.

The rain poured down across West Texas, filling Johnson Draw and sending a wall of water through Ozona on Monday, June 27, destroying property and claiming lives. Thirteen inches fell on the Sheffield area, where the river rose to a height of more than 17 feet. As runoff filled Live Oak Creek, the rising water gathered the dead brush and timber bulldozed over the past few years. When the growing volume of drift reached the Highway 290 bridge across the creek, it began to clog the waterway opening. Eventually, the pressure became too great, and the middle section of the bridge gave way. When it reached the mouth of the Pecos a short distance farther, the peak discharge was estimated to be about 100,000 cubic feet of water per second.

The Live Oak waters entered the Pecos, joining other floodwaters pouring into the river. Howard Draw, a seventy-seven-mile drainage that joins the Pecos just below the tiny community of Pandale, is fed by fifteen tributaries along its journey, all adding water to the raging draw. Five Odessa men who were fishing the lower end of the draw were trapped by the quickly rising waters. For several hours, they perched atop a pile of driftwood one hundred feet from the bank. When the drift broke up, they struck out for the shore. Only one of them made it. When found, he feared that the others were drowned. Horsemen riding through the deep mud eventually found all four alive.

At Pandale, another twenty-seven inches of rain fell, swelling the Pecos to record heights as it roared into the lower canyons. A wall of water eighty-two feet high reached the Highway 90 bridge near the mouth of the river at 7:30 a.m. that deadly Monday morning. The bridge was a five-hundred-foot Parker steel truss double span that stood fifty feet above the normal river surface. Built in 1923, it was the first highway bridge over the lower Pecos. The east abutment collapsed into the river. The eastern steel span was torn loose, its twisted remains carried one hundred yards downstream. The western steel span was also swept away, landing just off the west abutment. A car had stalled on the bridge in the rising waters.

Live Oak Bridge, destroyed in 1954 flood. *Author's collection.*

The driver led his family to safety and then returned to try to start his car when the water struck. A second crest of ninety-six feet arrived the following morning at 1:30 a.m., washing out the center pier.

The Pecos railroad high bridge survived the floods, but lower railroad bridges to the west were lost, stranding 264 passengers aboard the eastbound Santa Fe Sunset Limited in Langtry. Helicopters landing on the highway at Langtry carried the group to buses east of the Pecos.

The floodwaters entered the Rio Grande, threatening the border towns. Thirty thousand people evacuated the Mexican community of Piedras Negras. Floodwaters stood four feet deep on the main street of Eagle Pass. The fifty-six-foot crest of water continued down the river, where it washed out the center span of the International Bridge connecting Laredo to Nuevo Laredo. Falcon Dam eventually halted the raging waters.

Highway 90 Pecos River bridge, destroyed in 1954 flood. *Author's collection.*

Tuesday morning, the State Highway Commission reported an estimated $450,000 damage to West Texas bridges and highways. This did not include the projected $1 million cost of a new Pecos River bridge. The commission authorized construction of a temporary low-water bridge. Crews, working nonstop for fifty-seven days, constructed that low-water bridge, seven feet above the normal water level, with a "hair-raising approach." Plans were announced to construct a new permanent bridge, the highest highway bridge in Texas. Before work began in October 1955, Pecos River floods took the temporary bridge out three times.

Flood at Pecos Spring

Ethel Smith had lived at the old Sheffield homestead for sixty-four years when the rains began. She no longer lived in the original house built by Will Sheffield, but in the newer home next door. As she grew older, she did not spend the nights there, instead staying in town with her daughter at the old tourist courts. But the old place just upstream from Pecos Spring was still home to her. This rain would change that.

Ethel Kate Stubblefield Smith arrived at the Sheffield ranch in 1910, when she accompanied her husband, William Franklin Smith, there. They moved

90

their belongings and two young children in a wagon from Sherwood. When they started down the old wagon road above Fort Lancaster, Will locked the wheels. Ethel jumped out and grabbed young Pattie and Peck and walked down the steep grade with them. They crossed the Pecos bridge and rode upstream the short distance to their new home.

Will had been there before, herding sheep from the Sherwood, Texas area of Irion County. A young man of sixteen, he brought his flock to the Pecos River in 1886, camping near the spring. He did not stay that time, eventually returning to Sherwood and the beautiful Spring Creek Country.

Sometime around 1904, Will, now in his thirties, met a lanky seventeen-year-old. The Stubblefield family had recently migrated west from Liberty Hill, Texas, north of Austin, in search of new farmland. Will found himself attracted to this young lady and came to court her. When Ethel was working in the field and saw him riding up, she would cut across the fields to be at the house when he arrived.

The romance blossomed, and Will asked her father for Ethel's hand in marriage. Mr. Stubblefield thought that she needed to finish her schooling. Will saw less need for that. So, Ethel and Will and eloped to the Sherwood Courthouse to get married. She let him kiss her on the way there and then worried the rest of the ride that he would put her out of the wagon for being such a loose woman.

Six years married, they arrived at the old Sheffield ranch house, a short mile from the tiny community named for its builder. Together, they made the house—sitting low to the ground beneath tough hackberry trees, with its sandy-colored stucco walls, long front porch and high-pitched tin roof—into a home. They ran livestock (cattle, sheep and goats) on the rocky, mountainous, hardscrabble place. For many years, Will also leased the Pecos Spring land from owner John Cannon. The couple raised five children. They survived a depression, drought, two world wars and the loss of their youngest son to a bone disease at age nineteen. Their home became a social center for the Sheffield community, hosting family reunions and gatherings of friends, feeding folks in a long room on the back of the house or scattered around the yard, followed by lively visiting that lasted far into the night.

Will died in 1959. With her eldest son, Olin, managing the ranch, Ethel remained at the old home place. A new house was moved onto the property, and she moved in. The old place, however, remained filled with furniture, collectibles and memories.

In mid-September 1974, a cold front moved in, bringing more than a dozen days of rainy weather across West Texas. Five times the average

Will and Ethel
Smith. *Author's
collection.*

rainfall for the month blanketed the region, swelling creeks and rivers to flood levels. Some areas received more precipitation in a few days than they normally did in the entire year. Roads and highways became impassable at several points.

On September 21, the Pecos River crested at twenty-eight feet at Sheffield, coming within a foot or two of covering the Highway 290 bridge there. The waters spread across the river valley near Pecos Spring. When they reached the old Sheffield place, they surrounded the house. Several feet of dirty water and silt filled the rooms, destroying anything made of paper and soaking into walls and furnishing, warping, ruining. The new home received less flood damage, only a foot deep. As the rains continued for several more days, the floodwaters remained, wreaking more havoc on the aged structure. By the time they receded, the place was no longer habitable.

Ethel was visiting her daughter in San Angelo when her son brought the devastating news. When she was finally saw the damage firsthand, the shock was too much for her system. Medically, she had a heart attack or stroke, but more accurately, it was a broken spirit. She never recovered. Ethel died in the Iraan Hospital one month later, on October 28, at the age of eighty-six. The entire Sheffield community and people from miles beyond turned out for the funeral, held in the school auditorium, the largest building in town.

That old Pecos River killed Ethel as surely as if it had pulled her beneath its swirling, muddy waters.

IN A LONELY GRAVE

The couple wrapped the infant in a soft rabbit-skin robe, then in deer hide tied with cordage made from the mother's hair. They placed a cradleboard beside the bundle and covered everything with a finely woven mat of cactus fibers. With final loving care, they buried the child in the soft earth and ashes at the rear of the shelter, making this a special place. Many rock shelters along the Pecos contain similar remains of loved ones, those placed there always knowing they are not abandoned, but home.

Traces of graves remain along the river. Some still bear vestiges of information on stones or in historic accounts that preserve a fragment of the story of those who lie there. Others now mark lonely, forgotten lives of some of those who perished beside the Pecos.

A single grave lies on a narrow ridge overlooking the Pecos River canyon near where it meets the Rio Grande. The grave bears no name, no information about who lies there. Yet flowers have appeared on it from time to time. Are they from someone who knows the story of who is buried there? Or brought by visitors touched by this solitary grave in this starkly beautiful spot?

In 1854, young James Bell, a drover on a cattle drive to California, discovered an oblong pile of stones while moving cattle down Live Oak Creek. Another cowboy with him recognized the name on the inscription: "Amanda Lewis, 1852." Amanda was the mother of a large family from Mississippi. Bell mournfully considered how difficult it was for her family to leave her here. "In this vast expanse of hill and plain when by mere chance

Headstone of Little Margaret at Fort Lancaster. *Texas Historical Commission/Fort Lancaster State Historic Site.*

I came upon this grave a feeling of desolation and insignificance came over me." Sadly, Amanda Lewis's marker is now gone.

Nearby Fort Lancaster has a small collection of graves, several marked with small stones bearing no inscription. One likely belongs to Arthur, the fifteen-month-old son of Captain Arthur Lee who died in 1857. Lee was serving as second in command at Fort Davis at the time and returning to the fort when his party reached Lancaster, where the young child died. Nearby stands a weathered stone containing the inscription, "Little Margaret, Died October 13, 1858. Children are a heritage of the Lord." The rest of her story is lost.

Another Fort Lancaster grave has a bit more history. On November 19, 1861, Joseph H. Norris, a soldier in Company F, Second Mounted Rifles, died of pneumonia and was buried at the fort. One of his fellow soldiers, William Heartsill, spent four days carving the stone now marking Norris's grave. The inscription reads, "J.H. Norris, a W.P. Lane Ranger from Marshall, Texas. Died Nov 19th 1861 Aged 24 Years." Heartsill added, "This is covered with Glass and is set in the wall of stone, which is covered with cement, will stand for ages." Only the stone remains.

Charles Goodnight reported that there were thirteen graves at Horsehead Crossing, twelve of them from gun battles between cowboys. The tough cowman recalled, "I shall never forget the impression made upon me by those lonely graves."

Farther upriver and downstream in time, the little Girvin cemetery contains some forty rock or dirt mounds, most markers lost or rotted away with time. Among the few remaining stones is the small one for eight-year-old Ruth Ward, with the poignant note from her parents, "Daughter, we miss you."

Perhaps strangest of all the lonely graves is that of two-year-old Ellis. In 2001, residents in Iraan who were cleaning a flower bed in an old home realized that one stone was part of a tombstone. Searching the bed, they found a second piece of the limestone headstone. The inscription included the name "Ellis" and the information, "Born March 3, 1870, Died November 28, 1872." A triangular piece was missing where the stone read, "Son of…"

Investigation by Iraan historians brought no enlightenment. Nothing existed within miles of future Iraan in 1872. Despite speculation, no one has discovered who Ellis was and where his actual grave may lie. As local historian Edna Collett wrote, he remains a "little boy lost."

RIVER TOWN STORIES

The towns along the Pecos River in Texas, mostly located in the upper half of the river, each have unique characteristics, reflecting their origins. Founding communities along the river was never easy. Good water and land were scarce. Prosperity could be fleeting. Opportunity and fortune could fade with time or be quickly swept away. Like numerous unfortunate livestock at Horsehead Crossing, some perished, leaving their remains beside the river. A hardy few survived through a combination of gritty toughness and a bit of luck in the middle of nowhere, on the road to somewhere else.

Sandstone Quarry

The historic Ellis County Courthouse is considered one of the outstanding architectural structures in Texas. Stones from beside the Pecos River contribute to that fame. When architect J. Riley Gordon designed the courthouse to be constructed in the popular Romanesque Revival style in 1883, his conception called for using several types of stone with contrasting textures and colors. Among these were gray and rose-pink granite, limestone from Burnet County and red sandstone from the Pecos River Quito Quarry.

Building across West Texas in 1881, the Texas and Pacific Railway created stops at Quito for a section house and Quito Quarry as a water stop. Rock cut from that quarry still resides in historic buildings across the state.

Quito Quarry in 1895. *Ward County Archives.*

The exact details of the quarry's origins are lost, destroyed years ago in a fire. Whether the railroad helped establish the quarry or work had already been done there is unclear. An interesting tale, perhaps apocryphal, recounts that Jay Gould, the railroad magnate who helped finance the Texas and Pacific, stopped at Quito on a journey east in the 1880s. When Gould asked a local how the siding came to be, the man winked and stated that he had it built from stolen rails and cross ties to reach his quarry. In any case, only two years after the railroad reached Quito, the "Pecos" sandstone was already known widely enough for Gordon to specify it in his architectural plans.

Rock from the Pecos Red Sandstone Quarry was quite popular around the turn of the twentieth century. Besides the Ellis County Courthouse, completed in 1897, Pecos sandstone was used in courthouse buildings in San Antonio, Dallas, Lockhart, Jones County and Sulphur Springs. Closer to home, the first Ward County Courthouse, erected in 1893 in nearby Barstow, used the stone, as did the first Ward County Bank (1901), the Ector County Courthouse (1904) and the Midland County Courthouse (1905). Many of these structures are gone, the sandstone reused or discarded.

A layer of stone of a desired thickness was cut from the quarry and then carried to a metal building, where it was placed on a large wooden turntable mounted on wheels. The stone was turned, cut with large metal saws that sliced the rock into smaller blocks to ship out.

The expense of producing the stone contributed to the end of the quarry. Cement blocks could be manufactured much more cheaply. As building styles changed and demand for the stone decreased, the quarry closed in 1912. It was reopened a few times to provide new stone for buildings containing the red sandstone.

Some old timers believed that a Mr. McElroy was the quarry's first manager. Erving McElroy was born in 1879 and therefore too young for that position. He did apparently have a connection with the quarry. Although he spent much of his life in other occupations in Lubbock, upon his death in 1974, he was buried at the Barstow Cemetery. His death certificate listed his occupation as "stone cutter."

BARSTOW'S BAD LUCK

When the agricultural community of Barstow became the county seat of Ward County in 1892, its citizens dreamed of the town becoming an agricultural Eden on the Pecos. Extensive irrigation projects extended for miles up and down the river, with new ones planned or underway. In addition, Pecos sandstone from the nearby Quito Quarry was in high demand. Trainloads of stone regularly departed as construction materials for courthouses across Texas. Yet a scant fifty years later, all those dreams had, literally, turned to dust, and Barstow was a ghost of its former self.

Agricultural projects on the Pecos River began in 1877, but the 1889 law encouraging irrigation in the arid districts of Texas provided the impetus for Barstow. In 1892, investors established the Pioneer Canal Company around the future site of Barstow. Two years later, the enterprise became the Barstow Irrigation Company. George Barstow, author and pioneer of irrigation projects, served as company secretary. Trainloads of prospective settlers were brought to the company lands; many chose to stay.

In 1892, the townsite of Barstow became the first county seat of Ward County. A three-story courthouse made of red Pecos sandstone was constructed. By 1903, hundreds of acres of the Barstow Irrigation Company, stretching for miles along the Pecos, were under cultivation. Crops included grapes, peaches, pecans, celery, strawberries, pears and melons, shipped out in refrigerated cars cooled by ice from the Pecos Ice Plant. Cottonwood trees planted along the canals, together with vineyards and orchards, created shaded avenues, great for picnics.

Original Ward County Courthouse, built of red sandstone in 1893. The jail (*right*) was also made of red sandstone. *Ward County Archives.*

Barstow soon added an opera house, which hosted everything from amateur plays, parties and socials to imported professional productions. By 1914, the community had a school, three churches, a bank and a hotel. The population was a cosmopolitan mix of easterners, southerners and a few Californians.

Barstow grapes and peaches won four silver medals and a bronze at the St. Louis World's Fair in 1904. C.E. Peirce decided that his grapes would make a fine wine. He dug a large cellar and stored several casks there. When he believed that the wine had properly aged, he held a grand party with food prepared by an imported cook. To his dismay, all the casks proved to contain pure amber vinegar. Barstow failed to become the wine capital of the West.

In 1904, heavy rains upriver breached a dam above Carlsbad, New Mexico. A wall of floodwaters sped downriver. They destroyed the primary irrigation flume across the river and poured into the canal. Quickly overwhelming the canal bank, the floodwaters spread across the river valley.

As the alkaline waters receded, they left ponds breeding so many mosquitos that farmers wore veils to work the fields and even covered their horses' heads with nets or cloth. A salty residue soaked into the soil, permanently damaging it. The irrigated lands never fully recovered.

The vineyards and orchards were largely depleted by 1918. A shift to alfalfa hay and cotton, which were more salt-tolerant, helped for a time. However, drought and increasing dam and irrigation projects in New Mexico spelled the end of Barstow farming. The quarry had closed in 1912.

The 1920s discovery of oil in the Monahans area led to rapid growth of that community, while Barstow's population continued declining dramatically. In November 1937, an election to move the Ward County seat to Monahans won decisively. Barstow contested the result but lost again in a second election the following May. Less than a month later, the commissioners court voted to move the records. Five moving trucks waited outside Barstow, proceeding into town as soon as the vote became official. Under armed guards, "volunteers" quickly removed the county seal and records. A group of Barstow residents, themselves armed, gathered angrily outside. Fortunately, no violence erupted. The deed was done.

In one final run of bad luck, the Citizens State Bank of Barstow was robbed three times over a period of three years. A 1932 attempt by three bandits failed completely. In March 1934, thieves failed to cut their way into the vault, fleeing with only $36.10. A holdup man brazenly robbed the bank in 1935, escaping with $3,600. He was soon caught, and the money recovered, except for $10 he used to buy a shirt. Perhaps a total bank loss of $46.10 was not such bad luck after all!

Today, a few dilapidated homes and businesses along the old U.S. Highway 80 route remain as reminders of the grand dreams of Barstow's founders.

Legendary Pecos City

Pecos City arose on the west bank of the Pecos River with the arrival of the Texas and Pacific Railway in the summer of 1881. Built on dirty, chalky alkali ground "about as flat as a door," the new city of two hundred souls quickly gained a rowdy reputation. A group of Texas Rangers rode by in July 1881 in search of William Antrim, alias "Billy the Kid." Ranger lieutenant C.B. Nevill of the Frontier Battalion reported that, on their second night there, a local desperado fired into the Rangers' tents. Quickly disarmed, he was arrested, but with the justice of the peace seventy miles away, they released him.

By September 1881, Pecos City had 530 residents and six barrooms. Adobe was the primary building material. One visitor described it as "a small, straggling, lonesome-looking place in the middle of nowhere, full of Mexicans and wide-hatted, sun-browned, booted and spurred cowboys." Along with the saloons, there were a few small stores, several wagon yards and the big Johnson Brothers Mercantile.

Over the next decade, Pecos had its share of people of questionable or ill repute pass through or reside there. There were shootouts in the streets. You can still see the bullet holes in the floor of the Number 11 Saloon beside the Orient Hotel.

What gave Pecos its major claim to fame, however, was not desperados but cowboys. Pecos City, later simply Pecos, became the home of the first modern rodeo. If you search for the word *rodeo* in newspapers of the early 1880s, the term describes a roundup, usually a spring one. Cowboys from several ranches gathered to collect the cattle from the range, separate those belonging to their ranch and brand the young calves. The events certainly included demonstrations of roping and riding prowess, with accompanying brags. Impromptu competitions were a natural reflection of ranch work skills.

According to Pecos history (or perhaps lore), Trav Windham with the vast Hashknife Ranch and Morg Livingston of the NA Ranch, both with reputations as outstanding ropers, met up at Red Newell's saloon. Over drinks, they decided to hold a contest to determine who was best. Other cowboys heard of this and wanted to also demonstrate their skills. Local ranchers put up forty dollars of prize money. On July 4, 1883, the contestants met at a designated spot west of town. Spectators came from miles around, on horseback, in wagons, even on foot. Livingston and Windham each won events. The competition proved so popular that what is now known as the West of the Pecos Rodeo has been a nearly annual fixture of the community ever since.

Similar events sprang up under various names, including "cowboy carnivals." Other communities staked their own claims of being first. Eventually, "rodeo" was appropriated to describe a standard set of events involving both amateur and professional men and women competitors.

Some years at Pecos had unique contests. In 1929, the Pecos Rodeo included a one-hundred-mile race between the Thoroughbred horse "General" and Andrew Chimony, a Zuni Indian. A strained tendon forced Chimony to concede the race after twenty miles.

Pecos has grown into a more peaceable but bustling city of thirteen thousand people as part of the booming Permian Basin oil industry. However, the city has continued to embrace its rawboned western origins. The old

Number 11 Saloon has been preserved down to the bullet holes. The famous gunman Clay Allison is buried nearby. A somewhat incongruous replica of the Jersey Lilly Saloon stands in Centennial Park, a remnant from the 1936 Texas Centennial Celebration. Rangers rarely come to town these days in search of desperados, and there is a federal courthouse in town to dispense justice west of the Pecos.

DROVER'S PASS

Ernest Woodward believes that the family still has a drover pass somewhere. He just isn't certain which one of the brothers might know where it is. If he can find it, it may be among the last surviving ones from West Texas. Ernest is a third-generation member of a ranching family in the Girvin area and remembers hearing many tales of when the Pecos County ghost town just west of the river was one of the largest cattle shipping points in the United States and drover's passes were common.

Cattle ranches existed along the river beginning with the days of the open range in the early 1880s. The Union Cattle Company ran beef branded with a 7D along the west side of the Pecos from the New Mexico line to below Pecos Spring. As the open range era ended, families moved in, establishing ranches in the area. Virgil Nevill started his on the Pecos in 1906. John Girvin and his son Roy homesteaded four sections in 1907. Fonnie Woodward arrived in 1911 to work for local ranches.

Small communities, often no more than a general mercantile and post office, sprang up to serve the ranchers. The Adams Store opened a post office in December 1899 and operated until October 1903 along a mail route from San Angelo to Adams and on to Fort Stockton. A second post office named Phoenix started in 1910. Located in a dugout that also was a general store, it saved ranch families long trips to Midland to send or receive mail. Virgil Nevill posted his letter there, saying that he had married and that she was "a mighty fine little woman." The Phoenix Post Office lasted only two years, closing when the new railroad missed the community.

With the counsel of spirits he called "Brownies," Arthur Stillwell, a flamboyant Kansas City businessman, conceived the idea of creating a route from Kansas City, Kansas, to the Pacific Ocean at the Mexican port of Topolobampo. The Kansas City, Mexico and Orient Railroad, popularly known as the Orient, finally began construction in 1904 at Sweetwater,

Texas. Plagued with financial difficulties and poor equipment, the line struggled westward, finally completing a wooden bridge across the Pecos in 1912. A depot was established, originally named Granada. The stop was renamed Girvin for John Girvin. Financial difficulties halted construction to Fort Stockton for several months. The Orient would not reach the Mexican border at Presidio until 1928. The railroad never fulfilled Stillwell's dream of a major international trade artery.

The railroad did benefit Girvin, however. It ran through the center of the townsite, which soon had a store, hotel, saloon and lumberyard. Most importantly, a set of stock pens were built near the railroad. Ranchers along the western Pecos could now drive their stock to Girvin for shipping to points east.

Girvin also became a supply point for ranches farther downriver. Fonnie Woodward, now working and ranching south of Sheffield, used part of a World War I rolling kitchen as a chuck wagon. He hooked the two-wheeled wagon to his automobile for the fifty-mile drive to meet the train at Girvin. To guard against breakdowns of the old auto, he also brought two horses as spare power to pull the wagon.

Woodward and others drove cattle from Mexico and Pecos Country ranches to Girvin instead of Southern Pacific and Texas Pacific stops. With less passenger travel, the Orient gave right of way to trainloads of cattle

Girvin School House. The old Girvin Depot ticket counter is preserved inside. *Photograph by author.*

over all freight trains. This allowed a two-day trip between Girvin and the packinghouses in Dodge City and Des Moines, resulting in less weight loss of stock. Thousands of head of cattle left Girvin in the 1920s and '30s.

Drovers accompanying the cattle from loading point to packinghouse yards could travel free of charge with the cattle and on their return journey. A special ticket detailing this was called a drover's pass.

Cody Bell was a West Texas cowboy who rode the Orient on a drover's pass. Bell carried his saddle with him, loaded into a freight car. On the return trip, when he changed trains, the saddle missed the exchange. A local sheriff helped locate the missing saddle and reunited it with its owner.

A drover might choose to ride in the train's caboose, an option not requiring his pass. Some passes were thus carried home to the ranch as souvenirs. If the Woodwards have one of the old passes, it is a rare artifact.

In 1933, a new highway bypassed Girvin, the railroad moved south and the town declined. Today, only a few crumbling ruins remain along the old route. The stock pens are long gone. Only a few locals like Ernest recall tales of the days when trainloads of noisy cattle regularly rolled out of Girvin, the drovers onboard, passes in their pockets.

THE BIRTHDAY GIFT

The drilling crew drove the six miles to Ira Yates's ranch house to wake him up at one o'clock in the morning to tell him that they had brought in an oil well. The date was October 29, 1926. It was Yates's sixty-seventh birthday. He had just received an unimaginable birthday present. He went back to bed to sleep until his regular "getting-up time."

Orphaned at age twelve, Ira G. Yates Jr. worked digging peanuts and then as one of the youngest dealers in the purchase and sale of cattle, horses and mules. Working his way west from North Texas, he bought a ranch near San Angelo and continued horse trading but lost his capital in the Panic of 1907.

By 1912, Yates had recovered enough to buy a ranch in Crockett County. He also purchased a mercantile store in the town of Rankin, established in 1911 on the Orient Railway Line. When a rancher across the river in Pecos County thought that the mercantile looked like a prosperous venture, Yates traded him the store for the land, sold his Crockett County ranch and established his headquarters just west of the Pecos.

Ira Yates C-10 well blows in, 1927. *Author's collection.*

Shortly after 5:00 a.m. that morning, Yates and his son John drove over to Transcontinental Mid-Kansas No. 1-A Yates, a "rank wildcat." Things were quiet while Yates met with the crew until about 7:00 a.m., when the well began rumbling. Ira and John retreated a half mile from the well to observe. Yates later recalled, "In a little bit, oil came with a rush, throwing rocks out of the hole along with the gas and oil. It made a lot of noise and smeared the hillside for several hundred yards with oil. We did not know very much about oil, but we knew we had something."

The news spread quickly to nearby Rankin and McCamey and then beyond to the new oil towns across West Texas. Soon dust clouds marked the arrival of numerous automobiles as people came to see the new well. Yates began selling oil leases to eager buyers.

The well launched the discovery and development of one of the richest oil pools in Texas. By 1939, the Yates Field had 550 wells. Within a decade, the No. 1-A Yates had produced more than 2 million barrels of oil. The huge volume of production fueled the development of proration and new state and federal oil production policies. It forever ended the notion that there was no oil west of the Pecos and initiated the exploration and development of the vast oil resources of the Permian Basin.

When the well came in, the Yates headquarters became a boomtown of tents and shanties named Red Barn after the large red barn there. A few miles upriver, another more enduring oil community formed, taking its name from the Yates couple Ira and Ann Yates. Iraan continues to be a small but durable Pecos River town.

Yates became wealthy overnight. He was estimated to have received more than $5 million in oil royalties from the first ten years of production in the field. The orphaned peanut digger and mule trader died a wealthy man in 1939. Today, managed by technologies never imagined a century ago, the birthday treasure of black gold Ira Yates found beneath the rocky West Texas soil continues to be among the largest producing oil fields in Texas and the nation.

Red Lights Across the River

Grube certainly fit the image of a lawless place west of the Pecos. The only thing was that it lay east of the river, not west. Grube began as one of the most rapidly growing towns in the West Texas oil fields and just as rapidly came to an inglorious end. In its short life, it also garnered a highly notorious reputation.

On November 22, 1927, a little over a year after the Yates discovery well came in, Grube was established on a level stretch of land across the river from Red Barn. A group of businessmen from the oil boomtown of Borger formed the townsite company, named for B.H. Grube, one of the investors. They expected to profit when the new old fields extended into Crockett County.

By mid-January 1928, Grube boasted thirty businesses and a growing population, projected to reach six thousand by year's end. A thirty-room hotel was under construction, a modern affair with both hot and cold running water. The Griffith Amusement Company of Oklahoma City was erecting the $40,000 brick-and-tile Rex Theater, a motion picture and vaudeville house that would seat one thousand patrons. When completed, it was touted as the finest theater between San Angelo and El Paso. Water and gas lines were laid. A public school was opened. A bridge was built across the Pecos for access from the Yates field.

The town was billed as peaceful and quiet, perhaps as many as four hundred residents living there at the height of the boom. The *San Angelo Evening Standard*, however, commented that "the oil field worker can enjoy himself when he visits the little city." The peace and quiet quickly faded.

Grube's location in northwestern Crockett County placed it many nearly inaccessible miles away from the county seat of Ozona. A dirt road ran south for twenty miles to reach the Old Spanish Trail Highway, itself little more than a dirt and gravel road at this time. Crockett County officials were thus hours away. Some thought that they were perhaps paid to stay away. The bridge across the river provided easy access from Red Barn and Iraan, but Pecos County officials had no authority across the river. Essentially, Grube was beyond the reach of law and order and became a haven for bootleggers, showgirls and prostitutes.

The liquor and red-light trade catered to the oil field workers across the river, most of them single men or men away from their families. Grube came to life after dark. As the workday ended in the oil fields, open touring cars filled with enticingly clad women drove through the oil camps announcing music and dancing. As patrons crossed the bridge, which bore an advertisement for a funeral home, they were advised that they used it at their own risk. In this Prohibition era, bootleg liquor was so plentiful in town that the bootleggers wore identification to avoid selling to one another.

By November 1928, the situation was so bad that oilman Ira Yates and others convinced local Tom Brown, who lived in Crockett County, to run for constable of Precinct Three, which included Grube. Once in office, Brown did what he could to combat the crime. He would secretly enter Grube at night to find buildings with a storehouse of whiskey barrels. Crawling under the building, Brown drilled holes through the floor into the whiskey barrels. Angry bootleggers made various threats toward Brown, although his actions did little to stem the flow of illegal liquor.

Finally, the Texas Rangers were called in. Although no official records exist, residents were supposedly told to leave town. The Rex Theater was dynamited, scattering bricks in all directions. By May 1929, Grube was a ghost town.

The truth may be a bit more prosaic. Grube failed because the Yates field did not extend into Crockett County as hoped. Respectable folks moved to Iraan and other nearby oil towns. The speculators, bootleggers and dance hall girls moved on to new boomtowns. The *San Angelo Standard-Times* reported, "Grube is gone, and its chief bootlegger departed with only $12 in his pockets."

George Thompson filed paperwork to reacquire his land, and the Grube townsite reverted to pastureland. The remaining buildings fell into disarray, occupied by sheep, goats, rattlesnakes and lizards. The old bridge across the river fell years ago, and nothing remains of Grube save perhaps a few scattered bricks.

THE TIME MACHINE

Iraan built the time machine in the fall of 1965. With it, the city hoped to entice visitors to travel to a fictional past and, in doing so, create a greater future for the community. Although things didn't turn out quite as expected, they did produce a unique piece of Pecos River history.

Iraan came into existence following the explosive development of the Yates Oil Field along the Pecos in 1926. Everyone living there either worked for oil companies, such as the giant Marathon Oil, or made their living serving those who did. Since the town was founded on oil, it was natural that there would be an interest in the geology that formed these rich fields. The remains of ancient seas were easily visible in the surrounding mesas. Fossils of various ages littered the ground in many places. Some residents regularly collected them.

As they worked in the mesa country around Iraan, oil field employees also noted the remains of prehistoric people that were present almost everywhere. Mounds of burned rock, rock shelters with layers of ash and a variety of beautifully shaped projectile points lay among shining scatters of flint or chert. A group formed the Iraan Archaeological Society to more professionally learn and record what they found.

Among those who passed through the Yates field was V.T. Hamlin. While mapping oil fields there, he also learned of the rich prehistory of the region. When he later sought a career in comics, Hamlin drew on this knowledge to conceive a mash-up fantasy world. He constructed a "cartoonosaurus," a creature named Dinny unlike any actual dinosaur, who was befriended by the caveman Alley Oop. The resulting comic strip detailed their adventures in the kingdom of Moo, populated with an interesting cast of characters, including a curvaceous consort of Oop's named Oola.

To allow for greater range in his plots, Hamlin eventually brought Oop and Oola to the twentieth century via the time machine of Dr. Wonmug (a

Frank Balko working on Doc Wonmug's time machine. *Author's collection.*

parody of Einstein—"ein," one, and "stein," mug). This allowed Wonmug to send them into various adventures from ancient Troy to Arthurian England. The strip became a hit and has remained in print ever since.

Iraan had grown from an upstart oil boomtown into a prosperous little community by 1964, when Bernie Ayers, Iraan Christian Church's pastor, helped organize a chamber of commerce. To attract tourism, he sold the new chamber members on the idea of an Alley Oop Fantasyland based on Hamlin's comics. With Hamlin's blessing, the project was launched.

Drawing on their oil field skills and using local materials, Iraan citizens began construction of the new enterprise adjacent to the county park. With concrete and wire mesh, they erected an eighty-five-foot, eighty-five-thousand-pound replica of Dinny, which visitors could pose astride like Oop. Local artist Harley Brooks painted Oop striding across the tall sign above the gate to welcome visitors. In the center of the entrance, they built a small cinder block structure as Dr. Wonmug's time machine (although it hardly resembled the comic strip version). Adding various pipes, large insulators and other electrical equipment gave it a futuristic look.

Along with the park, Iraan leaders planned an annual event. On May 8, 1965, Iraan held the first Alley Oop Day. Events included a parade, an old settlers' reunion, performances by several bands and a Texas-sized barbecue. To entice even more visitors, the day incorporated two beauty pageants. A Queen Oola would be crowned from among young Iraan girls; surrounding communities could send contestants for Miss Stone Age. Hamlin attended as the special guest, posing beside Dinny bedecked with the youthful beauties. Sherry Chalfant became the first Queen Oola, and Big Lake's Jeanie Wright won Miss Stone Age.

The event proved a great success, enjoyed by both locals and visitors. Dinny became one of those weird roadside attractions folks would detour to see. The following year, Alley Oop Day included the dedication of a museum, constructed on the park grounds by the local amateur archaeologists and containing a collection of local prehistoric artifacts and fossils. Other activities included mule races, fireworks and, of course, a barbecue. In 1967, a twenty-five-foot Alley Oop bust, including his signature top hat and cigar, was added. A spindly metal rocket arose in 1970, promising "safe climbing" for children.

The park and the annual event continued for several years, but energy and enthusiasm eventually declined. Despite their creativity, Iraan folks discovered that building a theme park from the ground up became a daunting challenge. Aside from an old oil derrick and related equipment, little more was added.

Alley Oop Days have come and gone over the years, with events and guests varying. The beauty pageants survived for a time. The museum expanded its exhibits and operated for years but eventually closed. The rocket ship came down years ago. Dinny and Oop have endured, a bit weathered, requiring various repairs over the years. Tourists still stop by for photo opportunities.

The time machine remains at the entrance to Alley Oop Park, unrecognizable to any who do not know its story. Stripped of its exotic machinery, it appears to be a poorly placed storage unit. Yet as they walk around it into the faded glory of the park, visitors still step back to a space in time when Iraan dreamed big dreams of a Fantasyland.

BALLADS, MYTHS AND TALES

The Pecos River undoubtedly possesses a mythic element. Flowing between vastly different pieces of geography—the Llano Estacado, the Edwards Plateau and the mountainous Trans-Pecos—means that when you cross it, you arrive somewhere else geographically. Add the river's tortuous path (often encountered unexpectedly), dangerous crossings, unnavigable canyons and a region still largely empty of people, and it is easy to understand how the Pecos inspired a body of stories carved from imagination tentatively rooted in fact.

Some tales draw on the realities of the region, weaving actual locations and historical events and figures into their fictions, often taking great liberties with the truth. In true Texas-brag style, most exaggerate, often to the point of the ludicrous. Some are strange, some humorous and some beyond belief. Yet, however good the best of them is, they often pale before the real events of the place that inspired them.

THE PECOS RIVER QUEEN

Jack Thorp claimed that he composed his ballad shortly after supposedly hearing of the feat from Judge Roy Bean himself in 1901 while in the Lower Pecos country. He published it in his *Songs of the Cowboys* in 1908, with Bean no longer around to verify or refute the tale, having crossed the eternal bridge in 1903. Perhaps Thorp saved a legendary event from

Postcard of the Pecos River Viaduct. *Author's collection.*

oblivion, or perhaps he added his own creative tale to the classic folk songs gathered for the book.

The Pecos River Viaduct, the railroad bridge spanning Pecos River canyon more than two thousand feet above the water, was less than a decade old when Thorp wrote the song. Immediately famous as a spectacular construction, it provided rail travelers with an awesome, and perhaps a bit scary, crossing. Watching trains rattle across the spindly edifice, locals were equally impressed. It is not too great a stretch to imagine some old cowhands sitting on the rim and commenting, "Can you imagine riding a horse across that?"

A walkway with no guardrails ran beside the tracks, providing a possible horseback path. A few accounts, perhaps apocryphal, were told of some rider who crossed, clearly riding a horse with more sense than the rider. But a woman accomplishing such a ride? Now that would be a tale worth telling. That is the story narrated by "The Pecos River Queen." Accomplished cattle woman Patty Moorehead rode her horse across the bridge as a challenge to a lover.

N. Howard "Jack" Thorp became one of the earliest collectors of cowboy songs and poetry, beginning in 1899. Jack was an accomplished New Mexico cowboy and rancher, among other careers. He once bragged he had been everything except a telegraph operator or a preacher. Thorp's self-published 1908 book was the first of its kind, containing now classic songs such as "Little Joe the Wrangler" (written by Thorp) and "The Streets of Laredo." He sold them at cow camps, roundups and fairs. An expanded edition in 1921 contained more than one hundred songs, twenty-five written by Thorp, including "The Pecos River Queen" of course.

So, was there a well-known cowgirl who undertook this daring (and foolhardy) stunt? Does any evidence remain? Historian Mike Cox found a thread of Moorehead names—a J.R. Moorehead lived in Del Rio in 1900, and a Patty Moorehead Wilkins leased land near the bridge in the 1920s.

My own search through genealogy files yielded a James Moorehead who ranched in the area in the late 1800s who had a daughter named Ellen Patton, also known as Pattie, who was the wife of Fate Bell, who owned the land where the Fate Bell Shelter in Seminole Canyon State Park is now located. I found no evidence, however, that she was a renowned cowgirl.

Whatever the truth, the ballad of the Pecos River Queen has endured, set to music and sung by various balladeers. Thorp, Roy Bean and the viaduct are all gone, but the Pecos River Queen lives on in song. Here is her tale:

Where the Pecos River winds and turns in its journey to the sea,
From its white walls of sand and rock striving ever to be free,
Near the highest railroad bridge that all these modern times have seen
Dwells fair young Patty Moorhead, the Pecos River Queen.

She's known by all the cowboys on the Pecos River wide;
They know full well that she can shoot, that she can rope and ride;
She goes to every round-up, every cow-work without fail,
Looking out for all her cattle branded "walking hog on rail."

She made her start in cattle, yes, made it with her rope;
Can tie down e'ry maverick 'fore it can strike a lope;
She can rope and tie and brand it as quick as any man;
She's voted by all cowboys an A1 top cow-hand.

Across the Comstock railroad bridge, the highest in the West,
Patty rode her horse one day a lover's heart to test;
For he told her he would gladly risk all dangers for her sake,
But the puncher wouldn't follow, so she's still without a mate.

PECOS BILL

In the introduction to his 1937 Newbery Honor book *Pecos Bill: The Greatest Cowboy of All Time*, James Cloyd Bowman claimed that his work contains genuine American folklore. He asserted that the adventures of his hero "are collected from the annals of the campfire and the roundup." Well, not exactly.

Pecos Bill appeared a scant fourteen years before in a piece written by Edward O'Reilly for the October 1923 issue of *Century Magazine*. O'Reilly—author, actor and soldier of fortune—stated, "In my boyhood days in West Texas I first heard of Bill, and in later years I have often listened to chapters of his history told around the chuck-wagon by gravely mendacious cowboys." Well, not exactly.

The evidence is rather conclusive that Pecos Bill is based on little to no authentic oral tradition or historical prototype. American folklorist Richard Dorson classified Pecos Bill as "fakelore," an inauthentic, manufactured story presented as traditional and genuine folklore. Texas author, folklorist and authentic cowboy Paul Patterson claimed that Pecos Bill had to be fictional because he could do anything without putting a strain on himself. Said Patterson of Pecos River cowboying, "You can't do anything here without straining yourself."

Charles Doyle conducted an extensive study of Pecos Bill's creator and found roots of the character in the career of O'Reilly. O'Reilly wrote a somewhat exaggerated account of his service in the Spanish-American War in Cuba in 1898 that included serving under the commander of the American troops, Major General William Shafter. Prior to his service in Cuba, Shafter, a decorated Civil War veteran, served in various parts of the West, including Texas. While on a near-fatal trek in search of water, he earned the nickname "Pecos Bill" by insisting the expedition continue until reaching the Pecos, probably saving their lives. An 1898 ballad titled "Ol' Pecos Bill" enumerated the exploits of the famous officer, some of them fictional. The song described him as "a great big man with a great big heart, an' the proper sand in his craw." O'Reilly therefore most likely knew of this nickname.

Before the publication of his Pecos Bill tales in *Century Magazine*, O'Reilly wrote scripts and played in two silent western movies. In 1919, in *On the High Card*, he played a lawman facing the villainous character Pecos Bill. In *West of the Rio Grande*, filmed in 1921, O'Reilly becomes the villain Sinto, known by his alias, Pecos Bill.

Drawing of original Pecos Bill.
From Century Magazine.

While O'Reilly created Bill, James Bowman is responsible for the Pecos Bill known today. His book contains virtually all the heroic adventures generally attributed to Bill and his effortless ability to single-handedly invent the business of cowboying. Clearly intended for younger readers, the stories have a slightly humorous tone, even when describing potentially gruesome things, such as skinning cattle alive. Despite his rough mannerisms, Bill is an always virtuous gentleman at heart.

Compare that Bill to the original in O'Reilly's 1923 account. While Bill again invents most of the things connected with the cow business, he is also "the king killer of the bad men." His mother killed forty-one Indians with a broom handle and weaned young Bill on moonshine liquor. After his stint in the wild, Bill quickly learns to enjoy the vices of mankind. He becomes a bad man himself, inventing the six-shooter and train robbing, killing an unknown number of men along the way. Too civilized to scalp his victims, he simply skinned them gently and tanned their hides. He had a gift for profanity.

Some of his later famous exploits do appear, including fashioning a rattlesnake lariat, riding atop a mountain lion and a cyclone and digging the Rio Grande. He rides his famous horse Widow-Maker, who will have the ill-fated rendezvous with Slue-Foot Sue. Sue is only one of Bill's many love affairs, and he eventually shoots her to end her suffering aboard Widow-Maker. Supposedly he never gets over it, although he marries several women after that.

Bill's drinking finally kills him. When liquor becomes too mild, he turns to strychnine and other wolf poisons and adds fishhooks and barbed wire to the mix. The rusted wire eventually ruins his insides, sending him to "his infernal reward."

That was the original Bill, whose decidedly ambivalent career makes him more deserving of the nickname "Pecos" than the one found in children's books and Disney movies.

The Limestone Cowboy

Around 1980, Jerry Stone, an employee of Corvette Oil Company, was walking along the Pecos River near Iraan when he found an old, ragged, weather-damaged cowboy boot with a rubber sole. Stuffed inside was what appeared to be the bones of the lower part of a human leg and foot. Stone gathered up the grisly artifact and searched along the riverbed for other remains. He found none.

Stone carried the boot home to examine in more detail. The "bones" appeared white, at least on the surface, and hardened like stone. The lower portion in the boot was thicker than a human leg. The top of the material certainly looked like bone. Stone kept the "fossilized" boot, showing the strange find to others over the years.

In the late 1990s, Carl Baugh, a Young Earth Creationist, acquired the boot to add to his collection. Baugh contends that the planet and the creatures on it were created by the God of the Bible some six to ten thousand years ago. One tenet of this belief is debunking the idea that fossilized remains require thousands of years to form. A fossil foot in a cowboy boot seemed great proof of this idea.

Baugh investigated the boot and determined that it was possibly made by M.L. Leddy, the renowned boot company of San Angelo, Texas, that began manufacturing boots in 1936. When Gayland Leddy, a nephew of the founder, examined the boot, he recognized the pattern as the "Number 10 Stitch," used sometime in the 1950s. Thus, for Baugh, the cowboy's bone had "fossilized" in about thirty years.

Baugh added the bizarre item to his collection in the Creation Evidence Museum in Glen Rose, Texas, chartered "for the purpose of researching and displaying scientific evidence for creation." He stated, "The dramatic example of the 'Limestone Cowboy' immediately communicates the truth of the matter. Fossilization proves nothing about long periods of time."

Amateur paleontologist Glen Kuban, a skeptic of such matters, pointed out several problems with the fossilized cowboy story. Examining photographs of the artifacts, Kuban noted that the bones appear white, more typical of modern remains than fossil bones. A top view of the bones shows the internal structure of the bones with no indication of foreign mineral replacement of the spongy interiors.

Kuban pointed out that the material around the bone did not appear to have the shape of a human leg. Rather, it took the shape of the boot itself, the surface recording the contours and texture of the inside of the boot.

Petrified bicycle at Mother Shipton's Cave. *Wikimedia Commons.*

He concluded, "Rather than representing fossilized flesh, it seems more likely that the matrix around the bones is simply a natural cast of whatever sediment (probably a limy mud) filled the boot after the flesh rotted away."

Finally, Kuban questioned if the bones were even human. They appeared quite large in relation to the boot. "For all we know," he commented a bit sarcastically, "someone could have stuck some cow bones in a muddy boot."

Even if the bone is human, the more logical explanation is petrifying, not petrification. Petrifying is caused when an object is placed in water with an unusually high mineral content and becomes encrusted with mineral deposits from the water. The more porous the object, the faster this process occurs. Petrification happens when the molecules of the original object are replaced, not merely overlaid, with molecules of stone or mineral, a far longer process. Given the high mineral content of the Pecos River's mud and waters, a "petrified" bone, even a relatively recent one, is certainly possible.

In fact, you can find all sorts of "petrified" objects, from bicycles to teddy bears, at England's oldest tourist attraction. At Mother Shipton's Cave, open since 1630, the waters from a spring flowing over a large skull-shaped rock are so rich in sulfate and carbonate that things put beneath the falling water are soon "petrified." Every three to five months, a new teddy bear "fossil" is available for sale in the gift shop.

While there may be no prehistoric cowboy, there does remain the mystery of the foot in the boot. What strange misadventure befell some poor wrangler upstream—an accident on horseback, an encounter with a rattlesnake, a murder? While we may never know the answer, we do know one thing for certain. He died with his boots on.

DOWN THE PECOS

This river has it all—challenging whitewater, wilderness experience,
pictographs, petroglyphs, beautiful canyons and camps.
—Texas River Protection Association

PECOS RIVER FLOAT TRIP

Around 1900, J. Stokley Ligon and two of his brothers floated two
homemade boats from near the city of Pecos, Texas, to the Rio Grande
River. Once they passed the irrigation enterprises a short distance
downriver, the Pecos was largely uninhabited, save for a few hardy
ranchers. No written account of this remarkable feat remains. However,
in an effort almost as extraordinary as the trip, Stokley recorded their
adventure in a set of photographs taken with his new camera.

James Stokley Ligon was the second son of Seddie and Rebecca Ligon.
The Ligon family, including six children, had all arrived in Pecos County
in 1898, crossing the river by ferry boat near Pecos Spring. That year,
Seddie and his eldest son, Arthur, invested in a steam-powered water well
drilling machine, the first in West Texas. In 1900, they added a second drill
to the business. The Ligons drilled wells in several West Texas counties,
hauling the equipment back and forth across the unpredictable sands of
the Pecos River. In 1903, Seddie bought ranchland in Reeves County and

turned the water well drilling business over to his sons. Five generations of the family lived on this land into the twenty-first century.

Sometime during those busy years, three of the Ligon boys found time to embark on their journey down the Pecos. Stokley had purchased a camera by mail order in 1900. It was most likely the 1900 (5x7) field camera by Century Camera or one very similar. This camera, made of beautiful wood with a red bellows for focusing, was relatively small and lightweight and used dry glass plates, making it highly popular with amateur naturalists and landscape photographers.

The "dry" plates did not require development in darkness while still wet with emulsions. Their stability allowed for greater mobility and convenience. Photographers could wait to expose their plates and then store them back in the box until they could be developed. Nevertheless, glass plates remained fragile and surprisingly heavy.

As the Ligons loaded their boats with supplies (and a bicycle!), Stokley found room for his camera and an unknown number of glass plates. After the journey, the plates were developed and prints made. Stokley compiled them into a photo album (regrettably without captions) of eighty-eight images documenting their adventure.

The first few images capture the river's winding path across the edge of the plains. The earthen banks, ten feet or higher, lined with grass and scattered brush, are all that can be seen.

A small footbridge spans the river in an unknown narrow curve, perhaps near the old pontoon crossing at Camp Melvin, as the following image is identifiable as the old rock corral there. Next is what may be remains of the floating pontoon bridge built in 1868 to connect Forts Concho and Stockton. A panoramic shot captures a stretch of the river near the future site of Iraan.

Downriver, a shallow stretch of rapids grounded the boats, filling them with water, necessitating unpacking. While supplies and clothes dried on the bank, the boats were freed, and the men were once more underway. This would not be a solo event. There are several later shots of capsized and flooded boats and navigation of rocky passages. Viewing these, it becomes even more amazing to consider how Stokley managed to preserve both camera and glass plates.

The group spent some time at the ruins of Fort Lancaster, hiking up the old stage trail and photographing the ruins. At least five chimneys remained at that time. Only one remains standing today.

As the Ligons began their journey through the canyonlands of the Pecos, Stokley recorded the changing riverbank, photographing trees, springs

Ligon brothers on their Pecos River float trip. *Archives of the Big Bend.*

and the increasing height of the rocky canyon walls. The men took time for hunting and fishing. They posed with their guns at one spot. One of them stands beside a pole from which large catfish and waterfowl dangle. Another holds a large beaver. Two of the brothers appear to be dining well at the campsite.

After several scenic shots of the lower Pecos, they reach the Pecos River Viaduct. Along with shots of the full railroad bridge span, Stokley took detailed photographs of the stone pillars and the towering complex of iron composing the bridge. Then a shot of the old military road across the river, and they reach the mouth of the Pecos. The two rivers combine, unimpeded by the waters of future dams.

Undoubtedly, the Pecos River Float trip helped inspire Stokely's future career. He worked in wildlife conservation in New Mexico and Arizona, writing several books on the subject. He continued to purchase cameras, owning at least three in his life. His collection, housed at the Denver Public Library, includes 2,500 glass plates, nitrate and safety film negatives and 1,500 black-and-white prints.

Lower Pecos River Journeys

If you put your canoe or kayak in the river at the Pandale Crossing and paddle around the bend, you have committed to a journey of more than fifty miles across five days. Between there and the mouth of the Pecos is a pool and drop river, rapids, narrow limestone channels and stretches of boulders, the next challenge often hidden by tall reeds. The winds can be difficult, especially at the end. If the weather changes, the trip becomes perilous. There are only a few places to escape the high rock walls of the canyon, and those will leave you miles from anywhere.

A trip down the Lower Pecos is not for the meek. It requires good planning and preparation, including a careful reading of the guide by Louis Aulbach and Jack Richardson. Yet for those in good enough shape for whatever the river will throw at them, it's worth the effort. As Aulbach states, "The Pecos is a treasure that few people have had the chance to enjoy. [It] is a great place for solitude, but it is also a wonderful place to enjoy in the company of friends." Each journey has its own unique rewards and challenges, as the following accounts illustrate.

Vern Fish and friends Hank and Dan drove from Iowa in December 2018 for their river trip. As he ferried the group to Pandale, shuttle driver Emilio Hinojosa of Comstock recounted stories of previous trips that met various disasters, from broken ribs to busted boats. His last warning: have an escape plan if the river rises suddenly.

The group set out on a chilly 2019 New Year's Day. Within the first mile, Vern encountered the cane and ended up standing in the chilly river. He spent the remainder of the day fighting hyperthermia. By the end of day one, all three were wet and cold and made camp after less than five miles. After a night of freezing weather, the battered group decided to spend another day in camp to dry out and recover.

From that low point, the journey improved. "With the warm sun on our shoulders," Vern recalled, "the joy of paddling whitewater had returned." Navigating boulder fields and flutes, they took time to seek out some of the many pictograph sites along the river and climbed up to view the Lewis Canyon petroglyphs.

Bert and Dan Rodriguez nearly met disaster in 2014. On their third night on the river, rains poured down for hours. Shortly after dawn, waterfalls began flowing over the cliff edges into the rising river. Stashing their gear, the group searched frantically for an escape route, eventually finding a steep Jeep trail that saved their lives. The river rose thirty-one

Stokely Ligon photograph of the Lower Pecos, early 1900s. *Archives of the Big Bend.*

feet in an hour. The group lost more than $20,000 worth of gear, including kayaks and cameras.

Undaunted, they returned in August 2016, accompanied by Robert Field. Dan was armed with a satellite phone to receive weather reports. The trip started uneventfully. Field recorded, "The weather has been perfect, the fishing has been productive, and nobody has flipped in the rapids. Spirits are high." The nights were "magical." That would change.

Dan received a warning that a storm was approaching, and the group paddled hard for a safe campsite far above the river. Field was captivated by the lightning over the river and slowed to capture the best shot. Suddenly, his body tingled, and he was blinded by a blast of light. Realizing he had a near miss with lightning, he frantically paddled to escape the river. This storm proved less deadly than one in 2014, and with no more potential disasters, Bert and Dan, father and son, embraced. "We did it, son," Bert whispered. "We finished what we started."

In the spring of 2017, Pam LeBlanc gathered some friends for a trip down the river. One member of their group, Houston Dobbins, was a Comstock native and secured permission to visit special sites on the river. Having traveled the river multiple times, he even brought along his river dog Oso, who rode in the bow of Dobbins's kayak.

With a low river flow, group members were often out of the boats navigating shallow spots. The pace was a leisurely ten miles per day. The proprietors of J&P Bar and Grill in Comstock even delivered chicken tacos and cold beer on the last night on the river.

The final morning, a cold front dropped the temperature with a chilling wind. Cold and wet by the time they reached Painted Canyon and the largest rapids of the river, Pam decided to leave its passage to the experienced paddlers while she hiked around. Still, she was certain that Mother Nature had delivered the perfect adventure. "I'd trashed my straw cowboy hat, ripped apart one of my river sandals, and busted my sunglasses," she wrote. "We were tired and sunburned but couldn't wipe away our smiles as we pulled our boats out of the water."

GATHERING AT THE RIVER

O n an oppressively hot day in July 1864, Reverend Robert Lowry lay in his Brooklyn study exhausted from the heat. Almost incapacitated, he let his imagination take flight. Considering better days in the future, his thoughts turned to the book of Revelation in the Bible and the heavenly river—"the pure river of water of life, clear as crystal, proceeding out of the throne of God." Inspired, he composed the words of the hymn "Shall We Gather at the River?"

People have gathered beside rivers since the beginning of time. Uncounted numbers have come to the banks of the Pecos for myriad reasons. Some came on quests, seeking a sacred space to touch the spiritual. Some blazed paths along it, for glory or gain. Others made a home beside its waters. Many found it a seasonal space, a place to connect or reconnect with family, friends, tribes or traders to feast, to laugh, to mourn or to find solace. Hardly a beautiful, "shining river," its waters far from "crystal," even the uncomely Pecos has drawn a wide variety of peoples to its banks, brought there by some shared desire. And once there, they have found communion.

Old-Time Religion

The camp meeting is an old frontier tradition. In times when folks lived lonesome miles apart for months at a time, the camp meeting provided nourishment for the spirit and soul in ways far beyond the words of a sermon.

Farm and ranch families gathered at some special spot, often beside water. Everyone brought blankets or quilts to lay on the ground. There might be a few rough-hewn benches. There was preaching, sometimes several times a day. There were meals, often shared, perhaps beef driven there and cooked, along with special dishes, favorites of those who prepared them. Meetings frequently lasted several days. People slept in wagons and tents or wrapped in quilts under a blanket of stars. And there was communion, in all sorts of forms—religious discussion; sharing of news, both local and beyond; courting; laughing; bragging; and gossip.

The Pecos River Camp Meeting began on a different stream, although it flowed into the Pecos. Pioneer Terrell County rancher Charlie Chandler began ranching in the early 1900s along Independence Creek, a spring-fed stream in Pecos County that flows eastward to the Pecos. The creek delivers 27 million gallons of fresh water to the river, significantly improving the water quality. Chandler's ranch was a beautiful oasis in the Chihuahuan Desert country of the lower Pecos.

Charlie was a member of the Church of Christ, though not necessarily a church regular. As his granddaughter Charlena put it, "Believers [the Chandler family] may have been; churchgoers they were not." An important belief among the autonomous congregations of the Church of Christ is that one must confess belief in Jesus Christ and be baptized by immersion. Since cleansing of sins by total immersion was part of the salvation process, having a pool of water present following a profession of faith was always important.

Among Chandler's friends was Church of Christ Gospel preacher Dave Black. In 1940, Preacher Black attended a rodeo Chandler hosted on the Independence Creek Ranch. As the preacher observed the spring of cold water flowing nearby, an idea came to him. He told Charlie that this would be a great place for a camp meeting. Chandler agreed, and the idea took root. Brother Black soon recruited other converts to the cause. Sheffield merchant John Trotter, joined by local ranchers R.N. Allen and E.W. Hardgrave, helped promote the idea.

Chandler offered an old goat camp situated in a large motte of live oak trees for a site. The faithful, including many ranching families—the Owenses, Hardgraves, Trotters, Allens, Hales, Holmeses and Harrells among them—gathered at the creek, bringing camping gear and coal oil stoves. The spring provided fresh water. With no electricity, folks donated their cars for an evening to provide lighting. After the day's preaching, many headed to wade or swim in the creek or downstream to the Pecos to fish for catfish.

A second camp meeting was held the following year. World War II rationing and the call to duty for young men stopped the meetings. A desire to continue them persisted, however. Camp meeting leaders also wished for a more accessible site for campers.

That problem was solved when local church member H.M. Holmes and his wife, Johnnye, donated ten acres of land along the Pecos River beside the highway between Sheffield and the young oil town of Iraan. For the first meeting in 1944, a brush arbor was erected with a sawdust floor to keep down the dust. A generator-run Delco lighting system provided illumination for evening services. The site had no cabins or accommodations, but two hundred of the faithful again gathered for several days of singing and preaching, with baptisms in the Pecos. Sheffield Church of Christ minister James F. Black conducted services twice daily. The Pecos River Encampment was officially underway.

Meetings continued over the years, with Preacher James Black leading services even after he moved to Sterling City. New structures were added. By the fifth season on the Pecos in 1948, fifteen buildings had running water. A forty-by-sixty-foot steel and concrete tabernacle replaced the brush arbor. An open dining hall, stone tables and a mess hall could feed several hundred people. Peach, mulberry and pecan trees were planted for shade in the hot West Texas summer climate. A special bell now roused campers each morning, calling them to worship and sounding curfew each night. The "mellow toned" iron bell had hung over the dining hall of the Crockett Hotel in Ozona, built in the 1890s. When the Pecos River Encampment leaders decided to repaint the bell with a layer of aluminum paint, it destroyed the tone. Purifying the bell by fire restored the original resonance.

Eight hundred people attended in 1948, representing sixty-four towns from five different states for "preaching all day and dinner on the ground." Meals were free, provided by generous donations. Shirt-sleeved ranchers, aided by Mexican cooks, prepared three meals a day and served between three and four hundred attendees each meal. The menu was "ranch style cooking," with the main dish being barbecued goat. Several hundred loaves of bread, four tons of ice and one hundred Spanish goats fed the multitude.

The Pecos River Encampment has endured for decades, with folks gathering year after year. The technology—lighting, automobiles, sound systems—has all changed dramatically. However, there is still little or no cell service, which most consider a blessing. The number of buildings has grown, with some families even constructing permanent cabins. Trees planted in the 1940s now provide beautiful, shady groves. Barbecued and fried chicken,

Pecos River encampment tabernacle. *Photograph by author.*

ham and steak have replaced goat meat, but metal cans filled with ice still serve as cups at meals. The old bell is gone. A newer, larger one now calls to worship. The new tabernacle still has only a roof, with the sides open to views of the Pecos River Valley.

After a two-year shutdown due to COVID-19, the camp reopened. Two hundred people returned to meet old and new friends for a week of singing, preaching and barbecue. Although attendees now arrive from a technologically interconnected, urban world, much of the frontier encampment spirit remains. The reminiscence of Reul Lemmons, the evangelist who led the 1964 meeting, still rings true. "Cattlemen and sheep men and goat men squat in high-heeled boots in a close circle under the shade of a tree or in the blazing sun. They eat out of tin plates, and drink tea from a tin can as they discuss some Bible theme. Broad-brimmed straw hats—turned up on the sides and slid slightly to the back of the head—dip in agreement or shake in disagreement with a speaker's efforts."

Sitting at a summer evening service as the fading light of day paints the Pecos River Valley hills in shades of red and gold, the sounds of nature mingling with the fervent words of the preacher, it is easy to understand the enduring power of the camp meeting.

An Unlikely Course

Ranching has always been challenging in the Pecos River Country, even along the constant-flowing Independence Creek, but the drought of the 1950s destroyed many outfits and led second-generation rancher Joe Chandler to decide it was time for a change. He chose an unlikely course of action for West Texas, turning from livestock rancher to guest ranch host and counting on the stark, unspoiled beauty of the creek and the river to draw folks to come.

He began by digging a 40-by-120-foot swimming pool, constantly fed by flowing spring water. He traded some hunting rifles for enough cement to build a small store to supply fishermen coming to the river. The guest ranch amenities grew as Chandler erected cabins with water and electricity, creating space for more guests. He constructed ponds and lakes stocked with trout and catfish to attract more fishermen. As Joe later admitted, "I've done most of the work myself, just trying to make a living."

In 1954, he launched a campaign selling memberships for the private guest ranch. He had one hundred members in less than three weeks. To continue attracting members, Chandler continued making improvements. "I try to add something every year," he stated, "so if you don't like one thing, there'll be another." Options over the years included hiking, horseback riding and hunting. *Odessa American* staff writer Covey Bean described Chandler as a "Conrad Hilton of the Pecos [who] tried to offer something for everybody."

In 1965, Joe started work on a unique and ambitious "another"—a nine-hole golf course. Although he had never played golf himself, he knew that it was a popular sport among many of his friends and visitors. Encouraged by golfer Jimmy Attaway and with input from Bennie Adams, a pro on the course in McCamey, Chandler invested $30,000 to create a three-thousand-yard par-thirty-four course. He hauled in seven hundred loads of dirt for the fifty-five-acre layout, seeded the greens with special varieties of grass and underlaid the course with twelve thousand feet of irrigation pipe.

Completed in September 1965, the course was Joe's pride and joy. The only private course in West Texas, it quickly became popular with members and guests. Laid out through trees and across a lake, competent golfers considered it challenging. Joe joked that the lake, which blocked the approach to the no. 4 hole, contained more golf balls than fish. When he drained it in 1968, he took out eight hundred. Chandler took up the sport, and he and his wife, Mildred, spent time whenever possible on the course, growing into proficient players.

Maintaining the course required constant effort in dry West Texas. Joe passionately worked long hours to maintain it in pristine shape, with watering, fertilizing and mowing becoming daily tasks. Mildred pursued ground squirrels with her golf cart and .410 shotgun. Jackrabbits, cottontails and deer enjoyed dining on the greens. The occasional rattlesnake added an additional hazard. Javelina herds showed up from time to time.

When Joe staged his first semi-public tournament, the response was so overwhelming that he limited future ones to fifty qualified teams. Soon, local papers regularly carried the results of tournaments at Joe Chandler's Guest Ranch. Teams drove in from communities across the area. Players from the cities of Midland and Odessa drove more than 120 miles for the opportunity to escape the rush of these petroleum industry centers for a weekend. Teams competed in twenty-seven-hole low-ball partnership tournaments for top honors and merchandise prizes, with barbecue lunches for players and their families. Eventually, the ranch hosted four or five tournaments per year. Women's tournaments were added in 1968.

For the next thirty years, the golf course and the guest ranch were weekend or summer destinations for many West Texas families. Years later, John Walker, writing for the *Odessa American*, looked back fondly on those days, when a group of Odessa Jaycees headed south for "a weekend of golf and fishing and card playing and beer drinking while 'roughing it' in cabins complete with running water and electricity." Chandler family members toiled long hours in the evenings before tournaments preparing huge amounts of barbecued brisket and chicken and tubs of potato salad and pinto beans.

The tournaments proved quite profitable for Chandler. After the crowds departed on a Sunday evening, the Chandler clan gathered in Joe and

1980s photograph of the Whetrock Gang of Odessa, which organized tournaments at the ranch for several years. *Courtesy of Joe A. Chandler.*

Mildred's bedroom to sort and count the stacks of cash and checks on the king-sized bed.

By the late 1980s, Joe's health was failing, and the ranch had aged as well. By the end of the decade, it was closed and sat unused for the next few years. The golf course, left untended, began returning to a more natural, prairie-like state.

Fortunately, through an agreement with the Texas Nature Conservancy, Chandler Ranch reopened in 1991, with an emphasis on ecotourism. Special weekend rentals now include access to a variety of adventure amenities and country-style meals prepared by on-site cooks. It is a popular destination, and regular guests book stays well in advance.

Joe's golf course, however, returned to a state of nature. Deer and rabbits graze where golfers once lined up their shots. The golfing days of Chandler Ranch are a thing of the past. Only golden memories remain for those who once gathered beside the clear waters to play this unlikely course.

Pandale Buggy Run

Miguel Zuniga and Emilio Hinojosa await other arrivals where the Pandale road crosses the tracks of the Southern Pacific Railroad's Sunset Route. The tiny hamlet of Langtry, scattered down the slope above the Rio Grande River, is quiet. Only U.S. Highway 90 traffic breaks the silence. The morning is cool, although the promise of a hot June day is already in the air.

Vehicles of all sorts begin arriving, turning off Highway 90 or bumping over the railroad tracks from the north. Most are various side-by-side UTV (utility terrain vehicles) or ATV (all-terrain) buggies—a Polaris Ranger, a Honda Pioneer 1000-6, a Kawasaki Mule. There are a few pickups, some pulling trailers—even one motorcycle rider. Some vehicles sport U.S. or Texas flags. Most carry at least one ice chest of beverages for the journey. Drivers and passengers dismount, greeting their hosts and the other arrivals—some old friends, some new acquaintances. Whatever their chosen form of travel, they are all here for Miguel's somewhat annual "buggy run" to the Pecos River Pandale Crossing.

The run was mostly Miguel's idea. At least, that is how everyone remembers it, although loyal sidekick Emilio has been there from the first. As they recall, they were just looking for something to liven up the summer in Comstock.

The two are longtime residents of that small community (some four hundred-plus souls), twenty-eight miles east along U.S. 90, ten miles from the dramatic Pecos High Bridge crossing. Miguel is well-known around Comstock as a jack-of-all-trades, always active at some community-building project. He has held fundraisers for the Val Verde County Fire Department and the Val Verde County 4-H. He regularly organizes events for the school and the Comstock youth to raise funds or just create some fun.

Sometimes he sponsors an evening at the J&P Bar and Grill, Comstock's only restaurant. One of those interesting places you often find in an edge-of-civilization locale, the J&P serves amazingly good food (including especially delicious burgers) and functions as a de facto community center where locals mingle with visitors coming to boat and fish in Lake Amistad, the Pecos or Devils River. And as often happens in such places, one encounters a seldom-seen friend or relative. Miguel hires a local DJ to play and provides free food. The beer you pay for.

Searching for something else to liven up the summer, Miguel conceived the buggy run. A twenty-six-mile leisurely drive along the caliche county road running north from Langtry to where it crosses the Pecos River, with food and drinks to follow there. Anyone wanting to participate would meet at the railroad crossing with their chosen vehicle, mostly side-by-side UTVs or ATVs, and join the unhurried trek. Sharing the idea around Comstock and at the J&P, the word spread.

On a mid-June day some half-dozen or more years ago, the first run took place. A menagerie of vehicles arrived at the Langtry crossing—Comstock locals, other Lower Pecos residents and random folks from as far as two hundred miles away. The midmorning drive took over an hour, with the caravan spread out and traveling at a leisurely pace to keep the dust to a minimum. There were a few stops at the old shearing pens and before descending Little Fielder Draw to the Pecos, allowing time for passengers to share a beer or two and enjoy the starkly beautiful, arid Lower Pecos landscape.

A little before noon, the group arrived at the river. The road crosses the Pecos at a scenic spot where Howard Draw empties into the river. The riverbed becomes a large limestone slab providing space for parking and setting up shade tents. The shallow layer of water stretches downstream at least one hundred yards, filled with kids wading and ATVs sending trails of water sparkling in the sun. A deeper channel along the east bank creates several nice pools perfect for soaking in the cool river.

Over the following years, the basic plan remained the same. Each year, however, held its own unique features, the mix of participants always

Pandale Buggy Run at the Pecos River. *Courtesy of James Michael Collett.*

varying—some returning, some new. One year, Miguel brought a flatbed trailer, complete with generator-powered band, who played along the drive and at the river. Another year included a crawfish boil. During the pandemic, there was no run. Afterward, some years saw fewer buggies, but the ride has continued. At least for now.

This year, Miguel sets up a tent for shade and food for one and all. There is plenty of visiting, laughter and recounting of past years' adventures. Afterward, everyone chooses their own path. Some find a beer and a spot in the river. Some soak up the sunshine or lounge in the shade. Some have rental cabins at the nearby Pandale Crossing River Resort. Some wander upriver to fish. Time slows down—cell service is spotty or nonexistent. The only concerns are sunburn and running out of beer.

That may be the greatest reward of this simple event. To be completely present, to enjoy the moment, isolated from the cares, responsibilities and connectedness of the modern world. Cruising down the Pandale road in an open vehicle, one can almost believe the words of the Robert Earl Keen song. "The road goes on forever and the party never ends." Not quite, of course. Today, the road ends at the Pecos. The party will end with the weekend.

The Pecos, unmindful of this gathering as any others down the centuries, does flow on forever to its meeting with the Rio Grande.

Among the Spirits of the River

If you view the scene from the right angle, you feel like you have stepped into some strange time mashup. A collection of canvas tents form a line near the bank of the Pecos, occupied by a haphazard collection of soldiers, traders, schoolmarms and pioneers. A line of tepees sits across from them, stone tools, dried corn, hides and beadwork on display. Between the two, a row of cannons points across the river, which curves around the encampment, mostly hidden beneath steep earthen banks. A horse-drawn wagon rumbles past. A pair of Spaniards wander by in armor and conquistador helmets. The chuck wagons are parked a bit uphill from the river. The smell of horses, mixed with woodsmoke from cook fires, drifts across the site, mingled with the sights and sounds of crews hard at work cooking everything from coffee and biscuits to meat and beans. As you seek that perfect photograph that will capture these historic spirits from another century, you have to watch for the porta potties in the background, their bright plastic shells incongruous in the historic landscape.

For the last several years, different iterations of this collection of people have gathered at an unremarkable-looking spot on the Pecos River twelve miles northwest of Girvin to offer a free event celebrating Horsehead Crossing's history. The Pecos County Historical Commission claims that the crossing is the second-most iconic historical site in Texas. It may well be correct.

Almost every historic group and significant event of the Pecos Country's past, except oil, had a presence here. Native Americans, from ancient people with names now lost to modern tribes—Jumano, Lipan Apache, Comanche—all crossed here. Spaniards arrived, wandering into unknown lands eerily like their native Spain. Wagon trains bound for the California gold fields wrestled wagons across the swift and deadly waters. The Butterfield Overland Mail transported passengers across by ferry rather than risk their stages. Federal troops patrolled here. Confederates buried several compatriots nearby. Charles Goodnight and Oliver Loving blazed the cattle drive trail named for them, driving the first of thousands of heads of cattle into and across the muddy, rushing river. Gunfights and battles were fought here. Wealth, some real, some perhaps fictional, arrived here—wagonloads of salt, herds of cattle, silver, gold, rich jewels. The river swept lives, human and animal, away. Treasures were lost, stolen or hidden (or never there) in the mesa lands eastward.

In 2016, Betty Damron and other Crane County Historical Society members worked with Ernest Woodward, current landowner of the crossing's west bank, to hold a three-day celebration on the 150th anniversary of the 1866 Goodnight-Loving cattle drive to Horsehead and upriver to New Mexico. They formed the nonprofit Horsehead Crossing Goodnight Loving Trail Inc. to raise funds for a variety of activities, including bus tours to the crossing, a chuck wagon picnic and a special Fourth of July parade.

Inspired by the event's success, Damron and Woodward joined Pecos County Historical Commission members, including Kirby Warnock and Delane Cagle, to create a free public event bringing folks back to the river at the historic crossing. For two (and later three) days, they invited an amazingly diverse assortment of people to join them, as participants and visitors, to re-create elements of the history that transpired there. A central event would be a collection of chuck wagons feeding all present at no cost, although donations were welcome. Reenactors of all sorts, soldiers, pioneers and cowboys would create glimpses of life in another century. Native American tribes would come and share the lifeways and events of their people. Historians and archaeologists would detail events that happened there and point out traces remaining in the landscape. There would be music and cowboy poetry. Old-timers could sit and reminisce.

At the end of October 2020, the Horsehead Crossing Goodnight Loving Trail Inc. group raised $40,000 in funds and cautiously proceeded with the event, even as the fires of the COVID epidemic still smoldered. The brisk

Cannons firing at the Horsehead Crossing event. *Photograph by author.*

West Texas weather of the outdoor event provided some protection as folks spent chilly nights at the crossing in tents and RVs or drove in to wander the grounds, enjoying the historic mélange of reenactors, chuck wagon fare, cowboy songs, historic presentations and local craft vendors, all interrupted periodically by the powerful flash and roar of cannon fire. Despite the challenges, it proved a tremendous success.

Since then, the event has been held each year on the final weekend in October. An additional day was added for area schools to bring groups to experience living history at this place "in the middle of nowhere on a dead-end road on the Pecos River." Although the mix of activities and events varies, the chuck wagons remain a constant. In 2023, Comanche descendants of the famous Quanah Parker performed dances and shared stories, alongside Jumano and Lipan Apache tribe members. On Friday, the Natives invited several hundred schoolchildren to dance among them.

In past centuries, those arriving at the Pecos River encountered a dangerous, deadly place of passage and conflict. For the past few years in late October, Horsehead has become a place to gather, to hear, to share and, in a real sense, to experience the rich diversity of West Texas tales. Lipan Apache Richard Gonzales phrased it best as he recounted the grisly, yet ultimately triumphant, account of survival passed down from his great-grandmother through generations to him. Quoting his grandmother, Richard said, with feeling, "Remember, your stories make you strong."

BIBLIOGRAPHY

Austerman, Wayne R. "African American Troops of Company K, 9th Cavalry Fought in the Battle of Fort Lancaster." HistoryNet, June 12, 2006. http://www.historynet.com/african-american-troops-of-company-k-9th-cavalry-fought-in-the-battle-of-fort-lancaster.htm.

Austin American. "Noted Sheriff Beaten." November 4, 1926.

Austin Weekly Statesman. "Texas Facts and Fancies." September 15, 1881.

Baird, Bill. "Cosmic Road Trip: Located West of San Antonio, the White Shaman Is an Overlooked Texas Marvel." *San Antonio Current.* https://www.sacurrent.com/arts/cosmic-road-trip-located-west-of-san-antonio-the-white-shaman-is-an-overlooked-texas-marvel-27082147.

Bean, Covey. "Man in Black Tamed Brawling Fort Stockton." *Odessa American,* December 27, 1964.

Bolton, Herbert E., ed. *Spanish Explorations in the Southwest, 1542–1706.* New York: Charles Scribner's Sons, 1916.

Bowman, James Cloyd. *Pecos Bill: The Greatest Cowboy of All Time.* New York: New York Review Children's Collection, 1964.

Boyd, Carolyn. *The White Shaman Mural: An Enduring Creation Narrative in the Rock Art of the Lower Pecos.* Austin: University of Texas Press, 2016.

Boyd, Eva Jolene. *Noble Brutes: Camels on the American Frontier.* Plano: Republic of Texas Press, 1995.

Braudaway, Doug. "The Pecos River in Literature and Folklore." *Journal of Big Bend Studies* 18 (2006): 165–82.

Brownsville Herald. "Rio Grande in Record Flood." June 28, 1954.

Chandler, Charlena. *On Independence Creek*. Lubbock: Texas Tech University Press, 2004.

Collett, James. "El Presidente? Joe Madero of Sheffield, Texas." *Permian Historical Annual* 48 (2008): 5–23.

Collett, James, and the Fort Stockton Historical Society. *Fort Stockton*. Images of America series. Charleston, SC: Arcadia Publishing, 2011.

———. "La Frontera del Cielo." *Journal of Big Bend Studies* 14 (2002): 85–95.

———. *The Old Spanish Trail Highway in Texas*. Images of America series. Charleston, SC: Arcadia Publishing, 2021.

Conner, Seymour. "The Mendoza-Lopez Expedition and Location of San Clemente." *West Texas Historical Association Year Book* 45 (1969): 3–29.

Crockett County Historical Society. *A History of Crockett County*. San Angelo, TX: Anchor Publishing Company, 1976.

Daggett, Marsha Lea, ed. *Pecos County History*. 2 vols. Canyon, TX: Staked Plains Press, 1984.

Dallas Daily Herald. "End of Track." June 2, 1881.

Dearen, Patrick. *Bitter Waters: The Struggles of the Pecos River*. Norman: University of Oklahoma Press, 2016.

———. *Castle Gap and the Pecos Frontier*. Fort Worth: Texas Christian University Press, 1988.

———. *Crossing Rio Pecos*. Fort Worth: Texas Christian University Press, 1996.

———. *Halff of Texas: Merchant Rancher of the Old West*. Austin, TX: Eakin Press, 2000.

Dixon, Ann. "Letters from Texas: An Army Wife on the Texas Frontier, 1856–1860." *Journal of Big Bend Studies* 26 (2014): 181–97.

Downie, Alice Evans, ed. *Terrell County, Texas: Its Past—Its People*. San Angelo, TX: Anchor Publishing, 1978.

Doyle, Charles Clay. "Pecos Bill and His Pedigree." In *Celebrating 100 Years of the Texas Folklore Society, 1909–2009*. Edited by Kenneth Untiedt. Publications of the Texas Folklore Society LXVI. Denton: University of North Texas Press, 2009.

Eckhardt, C.F. "Remember Alley Oop? He's a Texan." Texas Hill Country. https://texashillcountry.com/remember-alley-oop-cave-man-texan.

El Paso Times. "The Pecos Viaduct." June 23, 1893.

Ely, Glen Sample. *Where the West Begins*. Lubbock: Texas Tech University Press, 2011.

Field, Robert. "Return to the Pecos." Duct Tape Diaries. https://community.nrs.com/duct-tape/2016/08/12/return-to-the-pecos.

Fish, Vern. "Lower Pecos River Trip Log." Canoeing. https://canoeing. com/lower-pecos-river-trip-log.

Flores, Rosie. "Ligons Honored as '99s Pioneer Family." *Pecos Enterprise*, June 29, 1999.

Fort Worth Star-Telegram. "Ira G. Yates, Oil Magnate, Is Dead at 79." April 13, 1939.

———. "Rattler, Lizard Keep Grube Halls as Boom Recedes." May 14, 1929.

———. "Record Flood Crest Rolls On to Laredo, Leaving Dead, Homeless in Its Wake." June 30, 1954.

———. "Road Losses Estimated at $450,000." June 30, 1954.

———. "Strained Tendon Ends Zuni Indian-Horse Race." June 23, 1929.

Francell, Lawrence John. *Fort Lancaster.* Austin: Texas State Historical Association, 1999.

Freitag, Ed. "Seven More Bodies Found in Flood Area." *San Angelo Standard-Times*, June 29, 1954.

Frohock, William T., Captain. "Report Being Attacked at F. Lancaster by 900 Indians on Dec. 26th. and Repulse of the Indians." Letter to Lieutenant John S. Loud, Ninth Cavalry Post Adjutant, Fort Stockton, December 27, 1867. Fort Lancaster, Texas. Letters Received, Headquarters, Fort Stockton, Texas, December 1867, NARS Microfilm Publication No. 1189, roll 2.

Fulcher, Walter. *The Way I Heard It: Tales of the Big Bend.* Austin: University of Texas Press, 1959.

Galveston Daily News. "The Pecos Flood." August 14, 1893.

———. "The Pecos Flood." August 10, 1893.

George, Olan M. *Roundup of Memories.* Seagraves, TX: Pioneer Book Publishers, 1987.

Gwynne, S.C. "The Lost River of Divine Reincarnation." Outside Online. https://www.outsideonline.com/outdoor-adventure/water-activities/ lost-river-divine-reincarnation.

Hale, Chris. "The U.S. Army Finds a Way: The Great Wagon Train of 1849." *Journal of Big Bend Studies* 30 (2018): 39–65.

Haley, J. Evetts, ed. "A Log of the Texas-California Cattle Trail, 1854, by James G. Bell." *Southwestern Historical Quarterly* 35 (January 1932): 208–37.

Hall, Winston. "'Pecos' Rich in Translation." Angelo State University Ram Page, September 9, 2003. https://www.asurampage.com/archives/pecos-rich-in-translation/article_898d08d4-0668-52f9-8b01-3963d549b2c1. html.

Handbook of Texas Online. "Fate Bell Shelter." https://www.tshaonline.
    org/handbook/entries/fate-bell-shelter.
———. "Howard Draw." https://www.tshaonline.org/handbook/entries/
    howard-draw.
Harvey, R.C. "A Stretch in the Bone Age: The Life and Cartooning Genius
    of V.T. Hamlin." *Comic Journal.* https://www.tcj.com/a-stretch-in-the-
    bone-age-the-life-and-cartooning-genius-of-v-t-hamlin.
Hickerson, Nancy Parrott. *The Jumanos: Hunters and Traders of the South Plains.*
    Austin: University of Texas Press, 1994.
Horn, Bob. "Iraan Getting Set for 'Alley Opp Day.'" *Odessa American*, May
    2, 1966.
Hughes, Alton. *Pecos: A History of the Pioneer West.* Seagraves, TX: Pioneer
    Book Publishers, 1978.
Kenmotsu, Nancy, and Douglas Boyd, eds. *The Toyah Phase of Central Texas:
    Late Prehistoric Economic and Social Processes.* College Station: Texas A&M
    University Press, 2012.
Kerr, John Leeds, with Frank Donovan. *Destination Topolobampo: The Kansas
    City, Mexico, and Orient Railway.* San Marino, CA: Golden West Books.
    1968.
Kilby, David, and Marcus Hamilton. "New Investigations at Bonfire Shelter:
    A Consideration of Bison Jumps and Their Implications for Paleoindian
    Social Organization." Paper presented at the 83rd Annual Meeting of the
    Society for American Archaeology, April 12, 2018, Washington, D.C.
LeBlanc, Pam. "Make a Date with Mother Nature." Texas Highways,
    July 2018. https://texashighways.com/adventures/make-a-date-with-
    mother-nature-on-the-pecos-river.
Leftwich, Bill. *Tracks Along the Pecos.* Pecos, TX: Pecos Press, 1957.
Lindsey, Ellis, and Gene Riggs. *Barney K. Riggs: The Yuma and Pecos Avenger.*
    N.p.: Xlibris Corporation, 2002.
Longfield, Kate. "Pioneer Woman Tells of a Perilous Trip." *Frontier Times* 14,
    no. 2 (October 1924): 56–57.
Luke, Clive. *The MUSK Hog Canyon Project, Crockett County, Texas.* Austin: Texas
    State Department of Highways and Public Transportation, Highway
    Design Division, Publications in Archaeology, Report No. 24, 1983.
Luna, Melinda. "Parker Trusses in Texas." American Society of Civil
    Engineers. https://www.texasce.org/tce-news/parker-trusses-in-texas.
Mallouf, Robert J., and Jennifer C. Piehl. "Woulfter Rockshelter: Preserving
    the Essence of a Late Prehistoric Mortuary Site in the Davis Mountains,
    Texas." *Journal of Big Bend Studies* 33 (2021): 143–86.

McAleese, Barbara E. *Echoes Along the Pecos River: Intriguing Ranch Tales from West Texas*. N.p.: CreateSpace Independent Publishing, 2014.

McCord, Marc W. "Pecos River." Southwest Paddlers. http://www.southwestpaddler.com/docs/riogrande10.html.

Moore, William E. "Archaeological Investigation at Musk Hog Canyon, Crockett County, Texas: A Report of the 1976 Texas Archaeological Society Field School." *Bulletin of the Texas Archaeological Society* 53 (1963): 13–81.

Munoz, Arturo René. "Fate Bell Shelter." Handbook of Texas Online. https://www.tshaonline.org/handbook/entries/fate-bell-shelter.

National Park Service. "Black Seminole Indian Scouts." https://www.nps.gov/articles/000/black-seminole-indian-scouts.htm.

Odessa American. "Alley Oop Park Reopens June 20." June 14, 1970.

———. "Spirit Remains Same at Camp." June 21, 1964.

Patterson, Paul. *Pecos Tales*. Austin, TX: Encino Press, 1967.

Porter, Kenneth. *The Black Seminoles: History of a Freedom-Seeking People*. Gainesville: University Press of Florida, 1996.

Pounds, Robert E., and John B. McCall. *The Orient*. Midwest City, OK: Santa Fe Railway Historical & Modeling Society Inc., 2011.

Powell, Eric. "Reading the White Shaman Mural." *Archaeology Magazine* (November/December 2017). https://docs.google.com/document/d/1e aIgFNWJyCXip1hPDv8w8KLqJmhHINW3QatbMQP0T9o/edit.

Powers, Andrea. "The Psychology of Rock Art." *Journal of Big Bend Studies* 20 (2008): 103–21.

Prewitt, Elton R. "To Jump or to Drag: Reflections on Bonfire Shelter." *Bulletin of the Texas Archaeological Society* 78 (2017): 149–53.

Ratliff, Ophelia Wood. "The Texas & Pacific in Ward County, 1880–1910." *Permian Historical Annual* 21 (December 1981): 97–109.

Roberts, Wilma. "The Petrified Lovers of Pecos: Vintage Yellow Journalism." In *Paisanos: A Folklore Miscellany*. Edited by Francis Abernethy. Austin, TX: Encino Press, 1978.

San Angelo Daily Standard. "Dud Barker Out After Two Decades as High Sheriff of Pecos County." January 2, 1927.

San Angelo Standard-Times. "Alley Oop Day Receives Iraan Prep." June 22, 1967.

———. "As Yates Extension Faded, So Did Grube." August 29, 1954.

———. "Edna Reed Clayton Dewees Obituary." January 25, 2009.

———. "800 People from Five States at Church Meeting." August 1, 1948.

———. "Pecos Bridge, State's Highest, Under Way." October 23, 1955.

San Marcos Free Press. "End of the T. & P. Track." September 15, 1881.

Schroeder, Eric A., Gary R. Perez and Joe R. Telez. "Written on Stone and Practiced on the Landscape; Pre-Contact Native American Cosmovision and the Sacred Landscape of the Edwards Plateau." *Bulletin of the Texas Archaeological Society* 92 (2022): 97–126.

Shumla Archaeological Education and Research Center. "About Us." https://shumla.org/about-us.

Skiles, Jack. *Judge Roy Bean Country*. Lubbock: Texas Tech University Press, 1996.

Smith, Dan L. *Texas Highway No. 1: The Bankhead Highway in Texas*. Fort Worth, TX: Bankhead Highway Publishing, 2013.

Smith, Julia Cauble. "Pecos, TX." Handbook of Texas Online. https://www.tshaonline.org/handbook/entries/pecos-tx.

———. "Yates Oil Field, Pecos County, Texas." *Permian Historical Annual* 31 (1991): 23–34.

Syers, Ed. *Off the Beaten Trail*. Fort Worth, TX: F.L. Motheral Company, 1964.

Tanner, Harold. "Tom Brown, a Bear, and a Town of Ill Repute." *Permian Historical Annual* 56 (2016): 19–32.

Taylor, Lonn. "Pecos River Flood of 1954." Texas Co-Op Power. https://texascooppower.com/pecos-river-flood-of-1954.

Texas Department of Transportation. "Texas Historic Bridges." https://www.txdot.gov/about/campaigns-outreach/texas-historic-bridges.html.

Texas Historical Commission. "The Battle of Fort Lancaster—December 26, 1867." https://thc.texas.gov/state-historic-sites/fort-lancaster/fort-lancaster-history.

Texas Rivers Protection Association. "About TPRA." https://txrivers.org/about-trpa.

———. "Lower Pecos River." https://txrivers.org/discover-texas-rivers/lower-pecos-river.

Times-Picayune. "Riding Westward on the Line of the Southern Pacific Railroad." August 18, 1895.

Toombs, Zane. "Small West Texas Town Produced State's First Female Sheriff." *Odessa American*, January 30, 2000.

Torres, Billy. "Something for Everybody at Alley Oop Day Festivities." *San Angelo Standard-Times*, August 14, 2023.

Turpin, Solveig, and Joel Bass. "The Lewis Canyon Petroglyphs." *Rock Art Foundation*, Special Publication 2, San Antonio, Texas, 1997.

Tyler, Ron, ed. *Wanderings in the Southwest in 1855 by J.D.B. Stillman*. Spokane, WA: Arthur H. Clark Company, 1990.

Uglow, Loyd. *A Military History of Texas*. Denton: University of North Texas Press, 2022.

Wallace, Christian. "Rodeo Is Like Religion in West Texas." Texas Highways. https://texashighways.com/things-to-do/rodeo-like-religion-west-of-the-pecos-rodeo.

Ward County Historical Commission. *Ward County, 1877–1977*. Dallas, TX: Taylor Publishing Company, 1977.

West of the Pecos Rodeo. "About Us." https://pecosrodeo.com/pages/history.

Whitehurst, A. "Reminiscences of the Schnively Expedition of 1867." *Southwestern Historical Quarterly* 8, no. 3 (January 1905): 267–71.

Willeford, Glenn P. "A Short History of Pecos Spring." *Journal of Big Bend Studies* 9 (1997): 69–74.

Williams, Clayton W. *Never Again*. 3 vols. San Antonio, TX: Naylor Company, 1969.

———. *Texas Last Frontier: Fort Stockton and Trans-Pecos, 1861–1895*. College Station: Texas A&M University Press, 1962.

Winpenny, Thomas R. *Without Fitting, Filling, or Chipping: An Illustrated History of the Phoenix Bridge Company*. Eston, PA: Canal History and Technology Press, 1996.

Woodward, Eddie Mae. "Girvin and the Pecos Country Before and After the Railroads." *Permian Historical Annual* 42 (2002): 93–102.

ABOUT THE AUTHOR

James (Jim) Collett is a native West Texan who lives in Midland, Texas. He has a Bachelor of Arts in history from Angelo State University and a Master of Arts in history from the University of Texas at Austin. A retired public school educator, Jim enjoyed his career working to share his love of history with teenagers. Jim is the author of five photo history books with Arcadia Publishing and has written several history articles for different publications. Jim is active in the collection, preservation and sharing of local history in Midland, including working actively in the development of the Midland County History Museum. In addition to his love of history, he is an amateur archaeologist who has spent many enjoyable hours wandering the West Texas landscape along the Pecos River and beyond. Jim is also a member of the Texas Rivers Protection Association.